THE PETROGLYPH COLORING BOOK

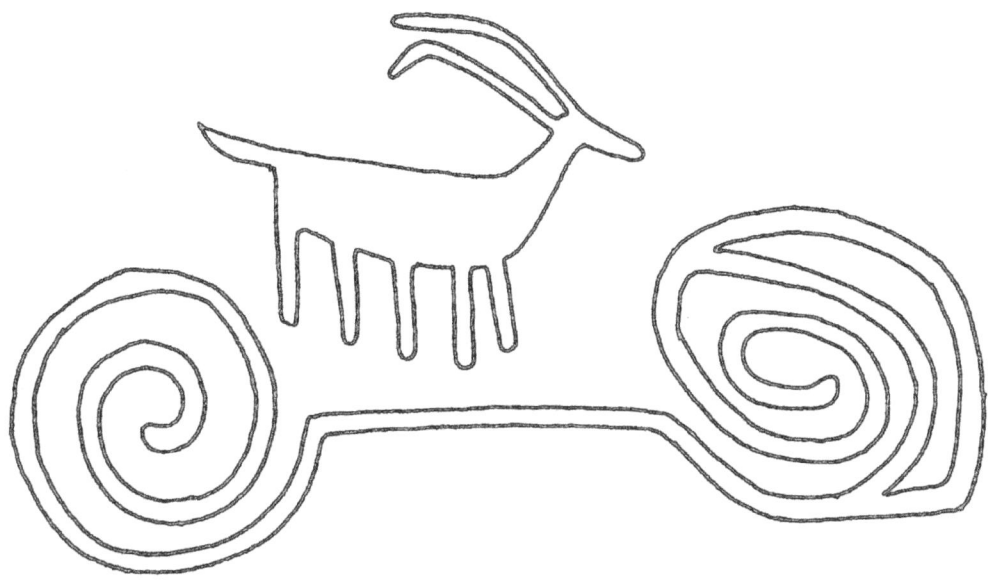

Pat Preble

Illustrated by Deborah Harmon

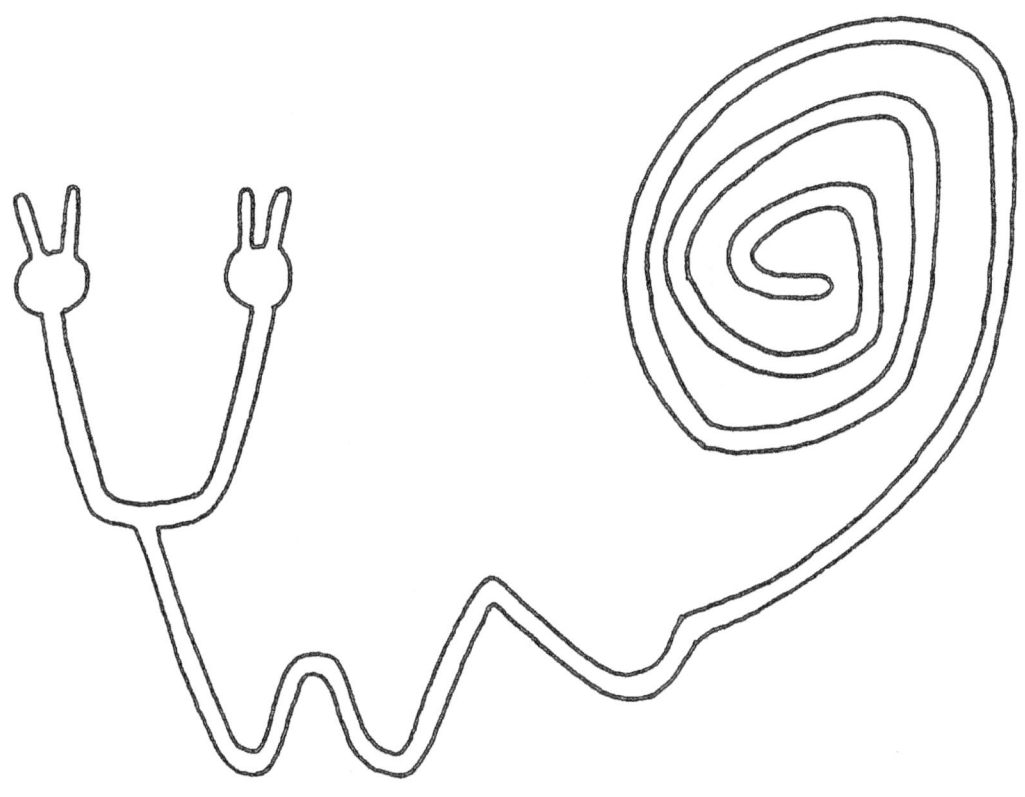

Copyright
Copyright ©2016 by Patricia Preble

Published through CreateSpace, an Amazon company
ISBN-13: 9781533088383
ISBN-10: 1533088381

Contact: Info@PatPreble.com
www.patpreble.com

What is a Petroglyph?

'Petro' was derived from Greek and means stone or rock and 'glyph' is also Greek. It means to hollow out or carve; thus, petroglyph means image carved on a rock. Petroglyphs can be found all over the southwestern United States (and many other places in the world as well). Along the 17 mile escarpment at the New Mexico Petroglyph National Monument there are approximately 25,000 petroglyph images. The creation dates for those images range from B.C. 2000 up through the late 1680s. If you are interested in seeing images of the actual sites, try searching online for "Native American Rock Art", or "Petroglyph Sites". Quite a few sites will pop up showing rock art from California, Nevada, and New Mexico.

No one knows why the ancient petroglyph images were made. And no one today knows what they mean. Recently there have been speculations by anthropologists that the drawings were traced by Shamans as part of their vision quest trances. (For brilliant insights into the possible meanings of rock art, see the writings of David S. Whitley; and, also, J.D. Lewis-Williams,).

It is a curious thing how an image can interact with the subconscious mind. All of the innovations that I have made with the encaustic painting medium have come about after my having worked with the petroglyph images. Every time I work with the images, major shifts of understanding and new directions take place in my painting. It makes me wonder if these images are possibly very powerful notes from the past? Notes that can inspire deeper understanding?

The images are presented here for your perusal. Look at them, color them, and, especially, relax and enjoy the quiet moments of simple engagement in the process of your creativity.

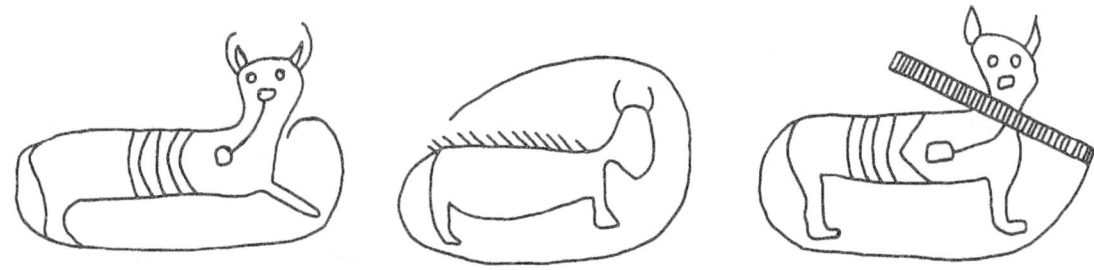

Some ideas for how to color in this book

The easiest method for coloring the images in this book is to use one color on the inside of the petroglyph and use a different color on the paper around the petroglyph.

If you want to get more involved, you could draw a rough line around a petroglyph. (Fig. 1)

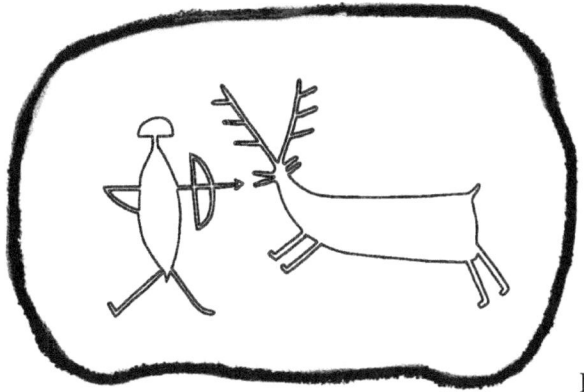

Fig. 1

Get some coarse sandpaper and put it under the page you are coloring on. Lightly color over the page with a crayon of your choice (called "burnishing"). The crayon will pick up the texture of the sandpaper and create a rock-like look to the page. With sandpaper underneath the page use a crayon to burnish color outside the line. (Fig. 2)

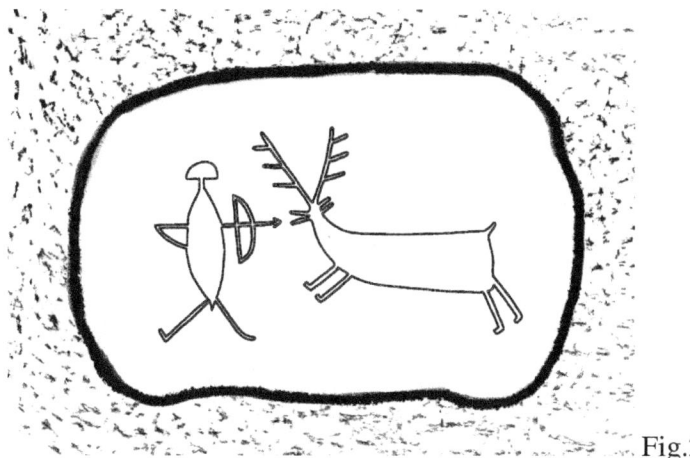

Fig.2

Next, remove the coarse sandpaper and put a fine grade of sandpaper under the page. Choose a new color, or the same color, and burnish the page inside the rock creating a different color and texture for the picture. (Fig. 3)

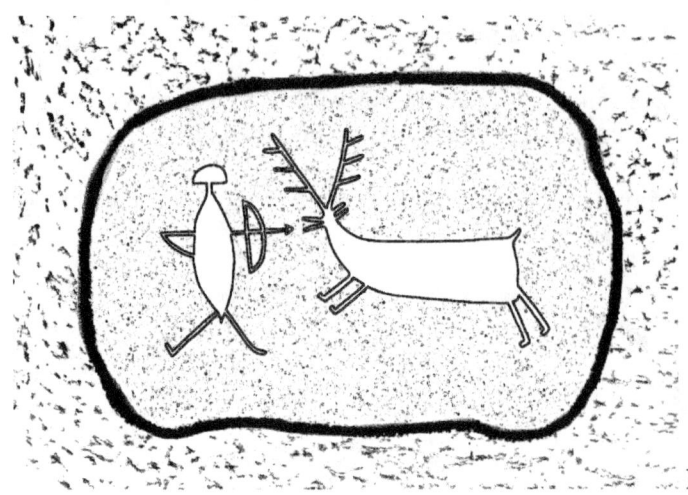

Fig. 3

You can have a lot of fun with this burnishing technique.

You could leave the coarse sand paper in and choose a different color for inside the line.

You could insert finer grade sandpaper and then burnish with a different color over the same area where the coarse sandpaper was burnished to get a two dimensional layer of grain.

You could dispense with the line around the petroglyph and just color the page with various color burnishings. (Fig. 4)

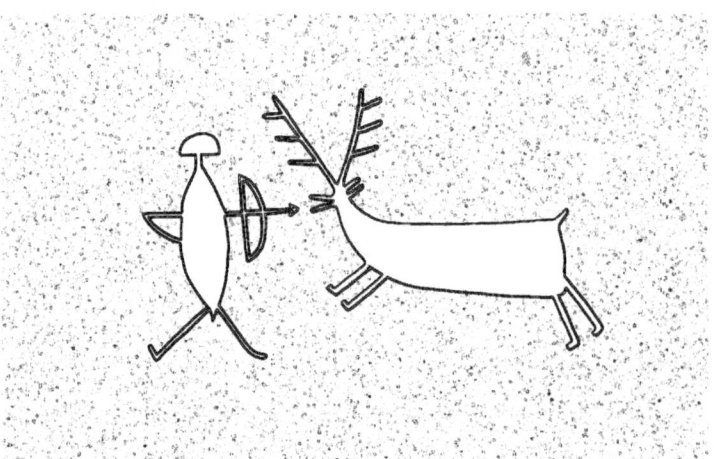

Fig. 4

Rocks in the desert are very colorful; rust, orange, red, yellow, ochre, and then there are green lichens that form on the rocks. Pinks and purples work well too.

Let your imagination and creativity run free.

4

Debbie's Petroglyph Drawings

(There are no page numbers on the petroglyph pages.)

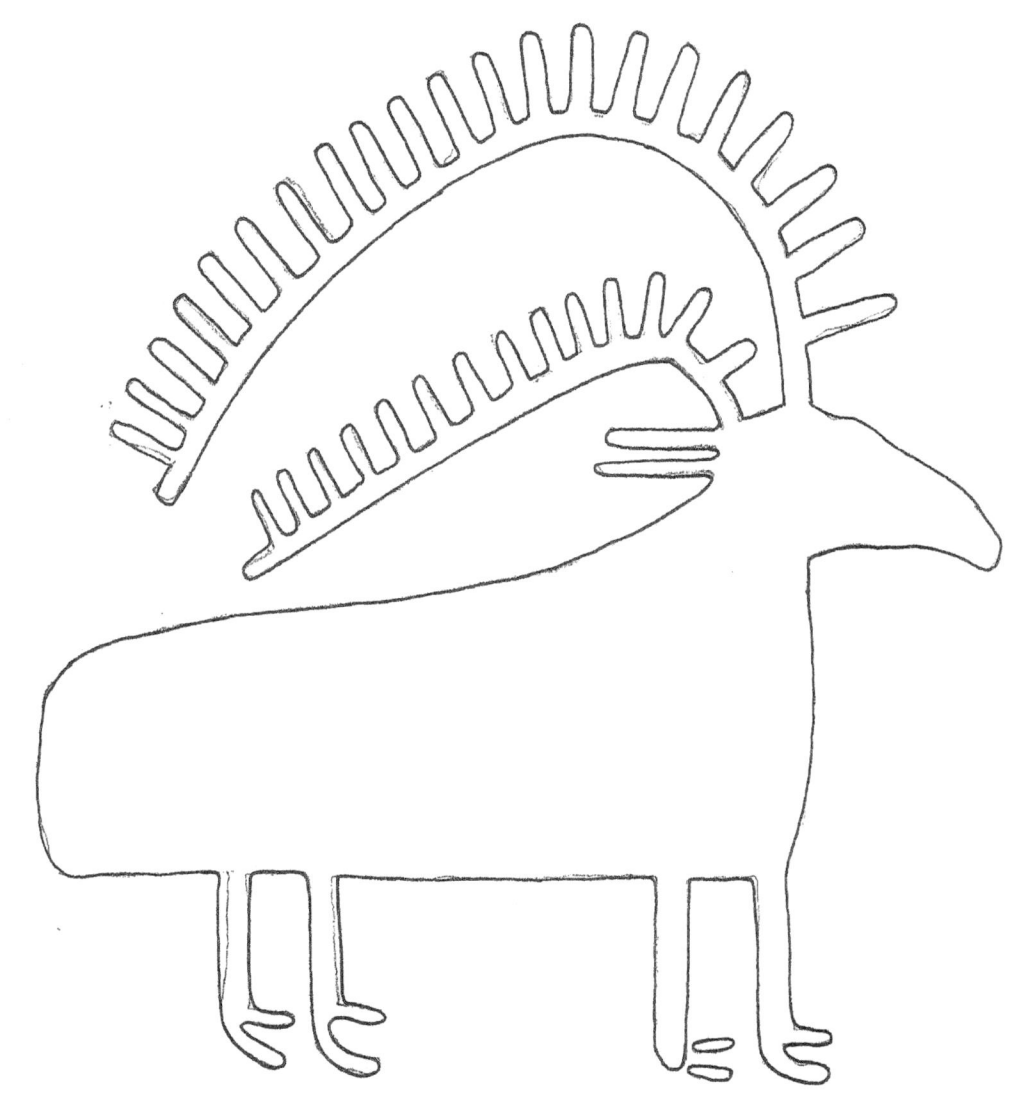

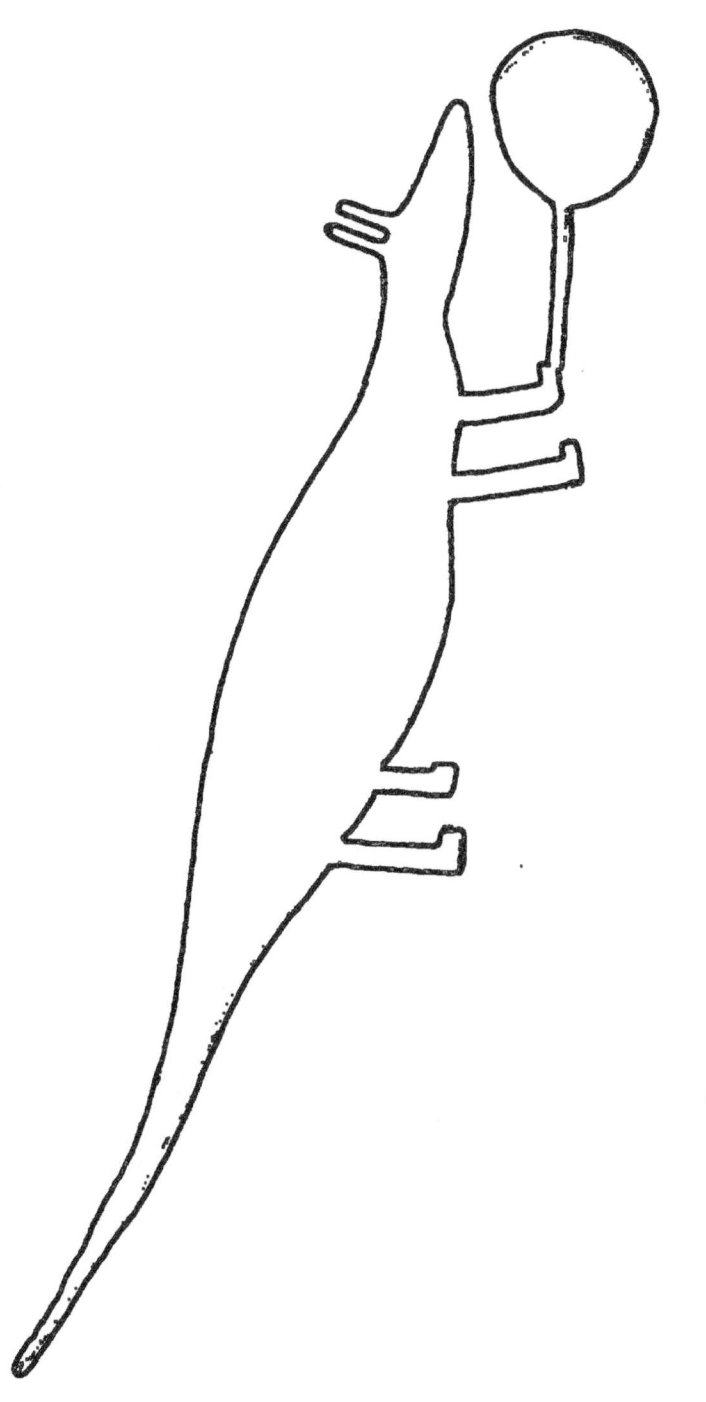

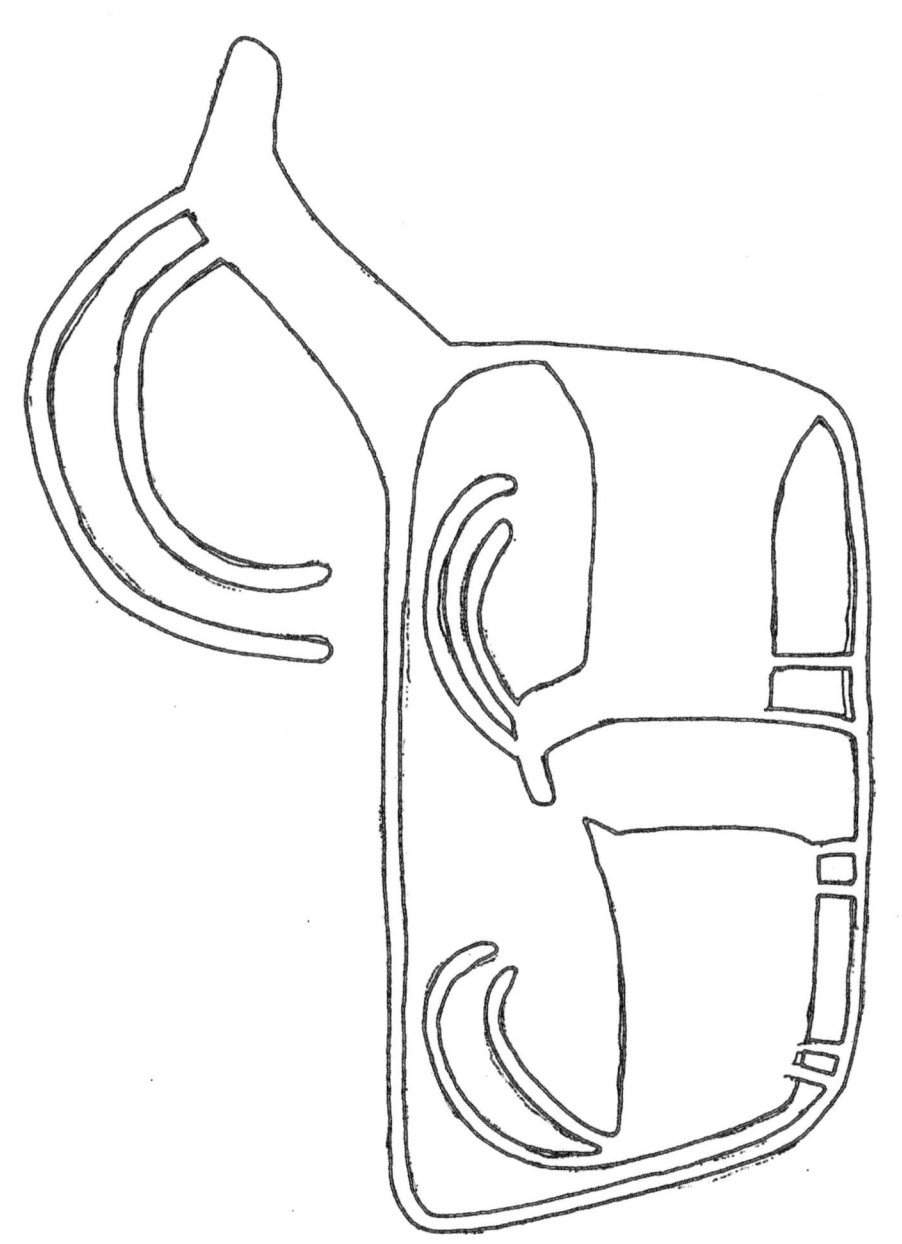

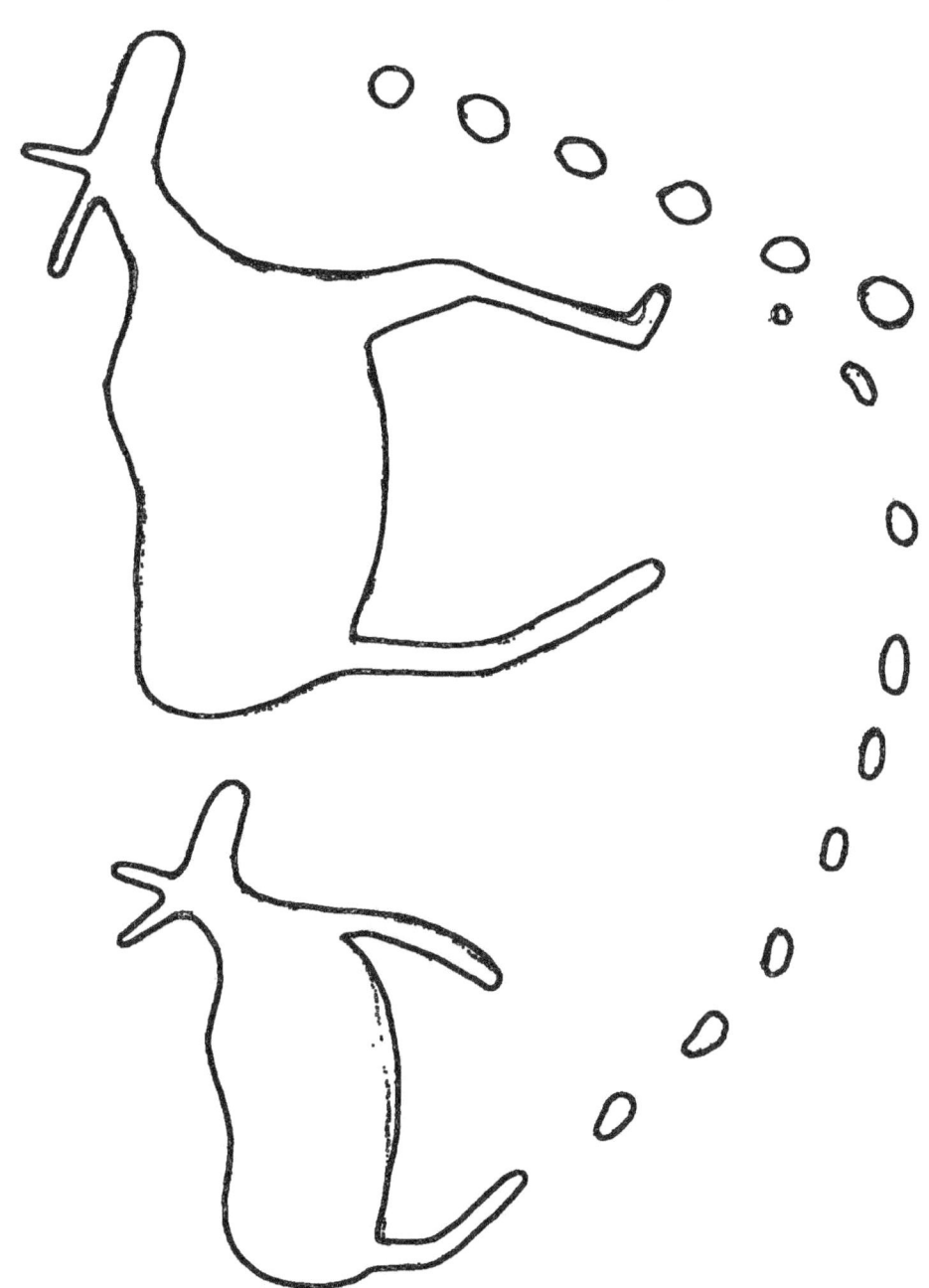

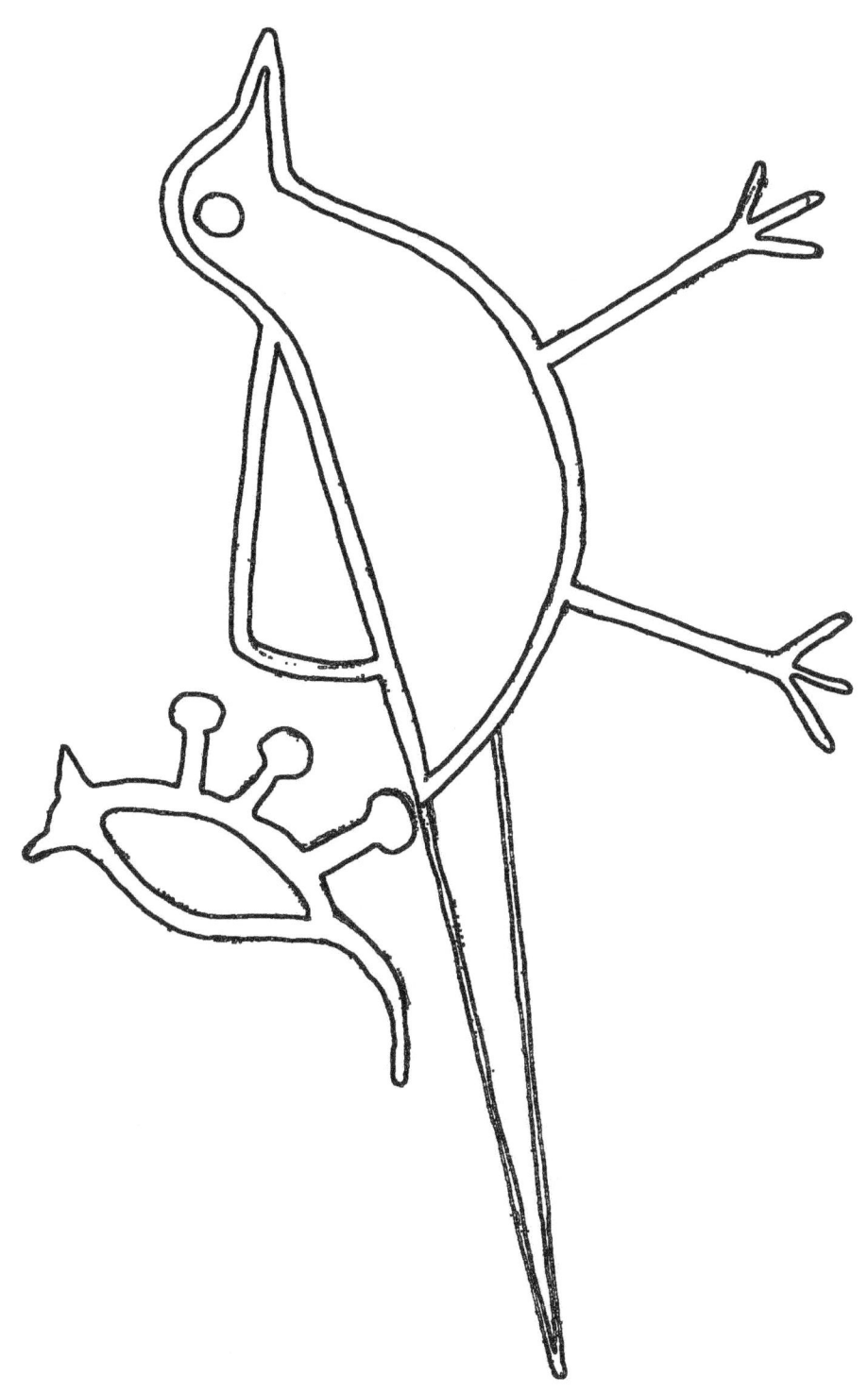

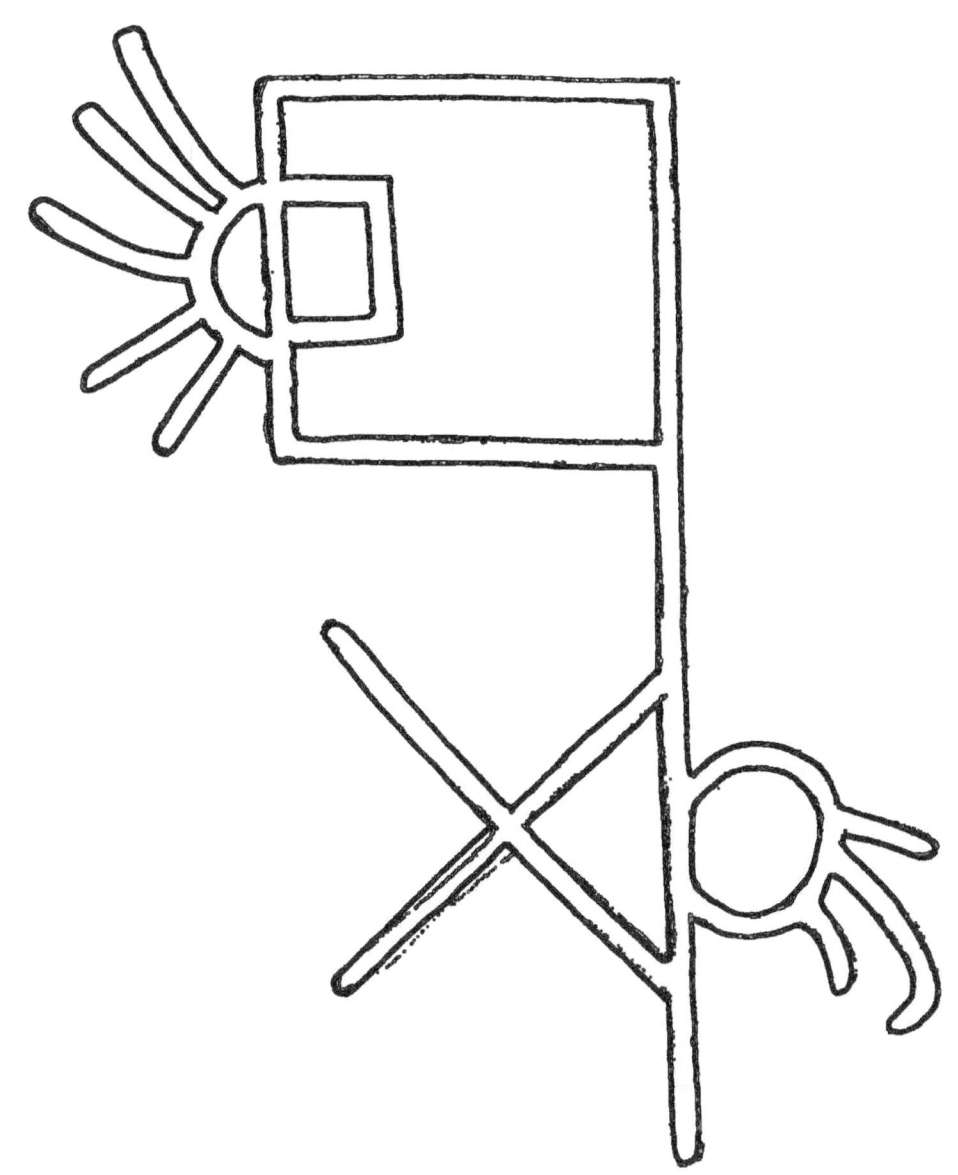

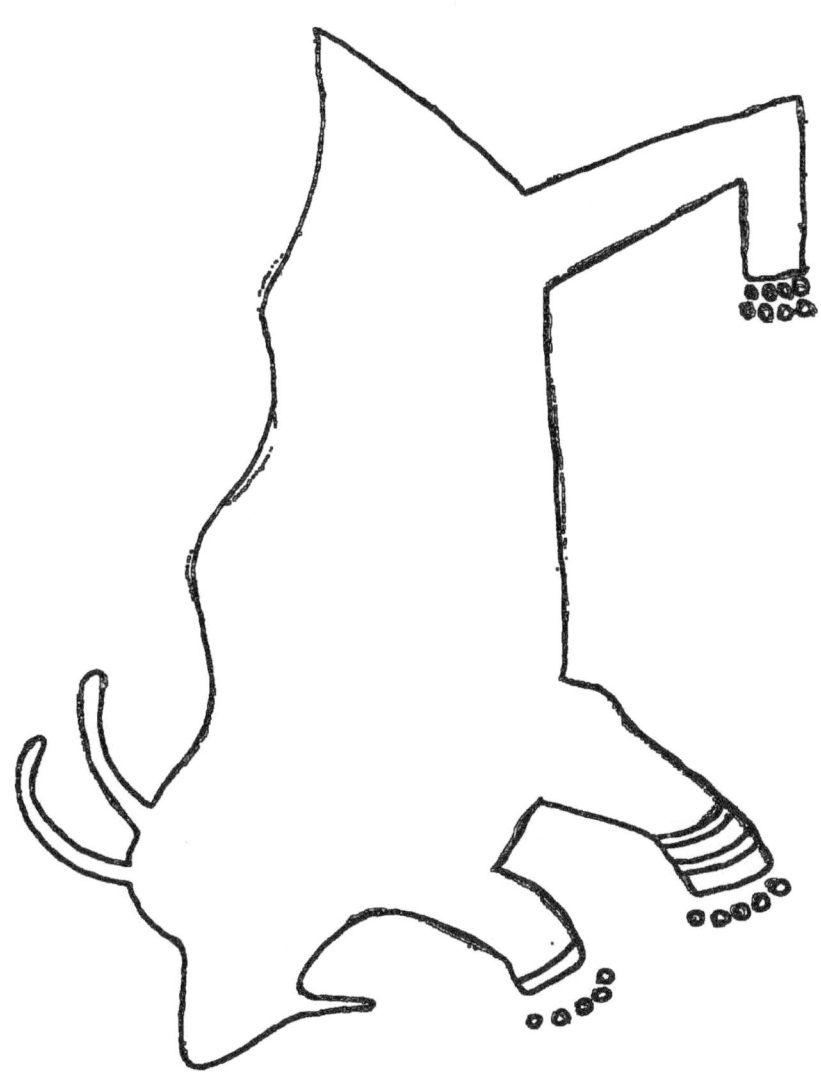

20

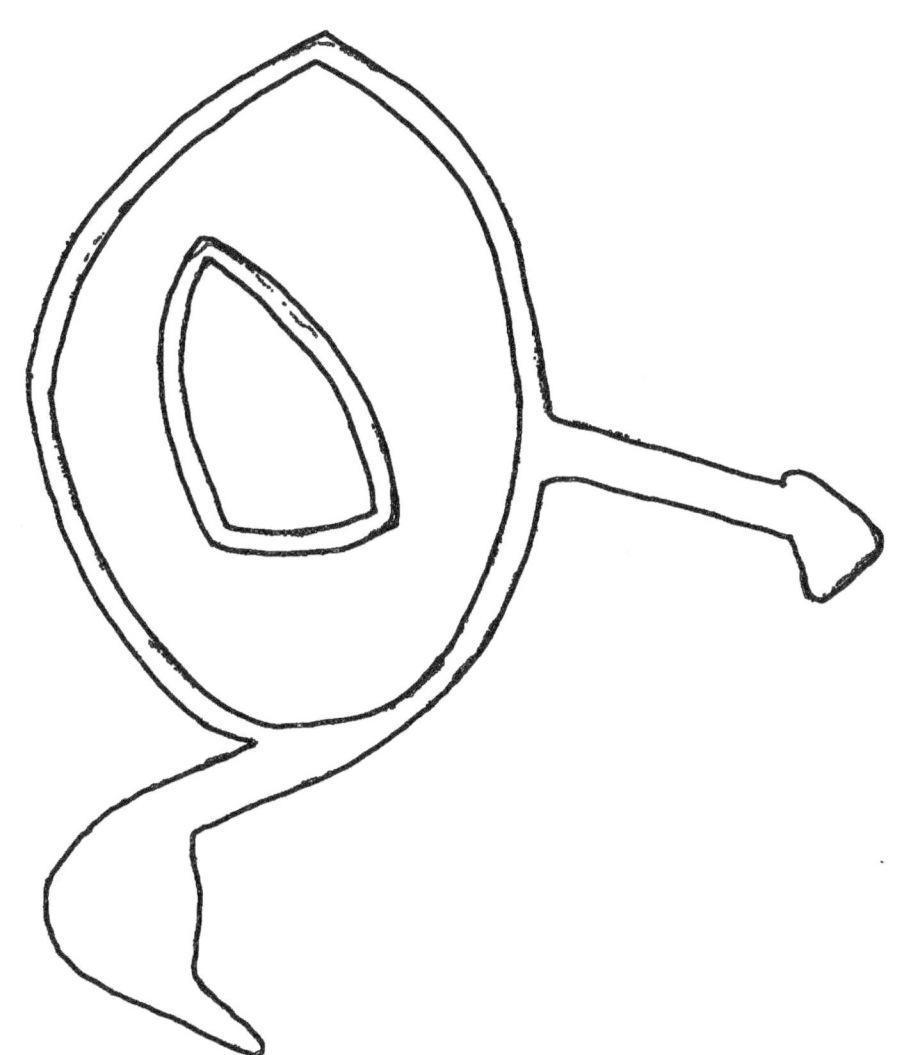

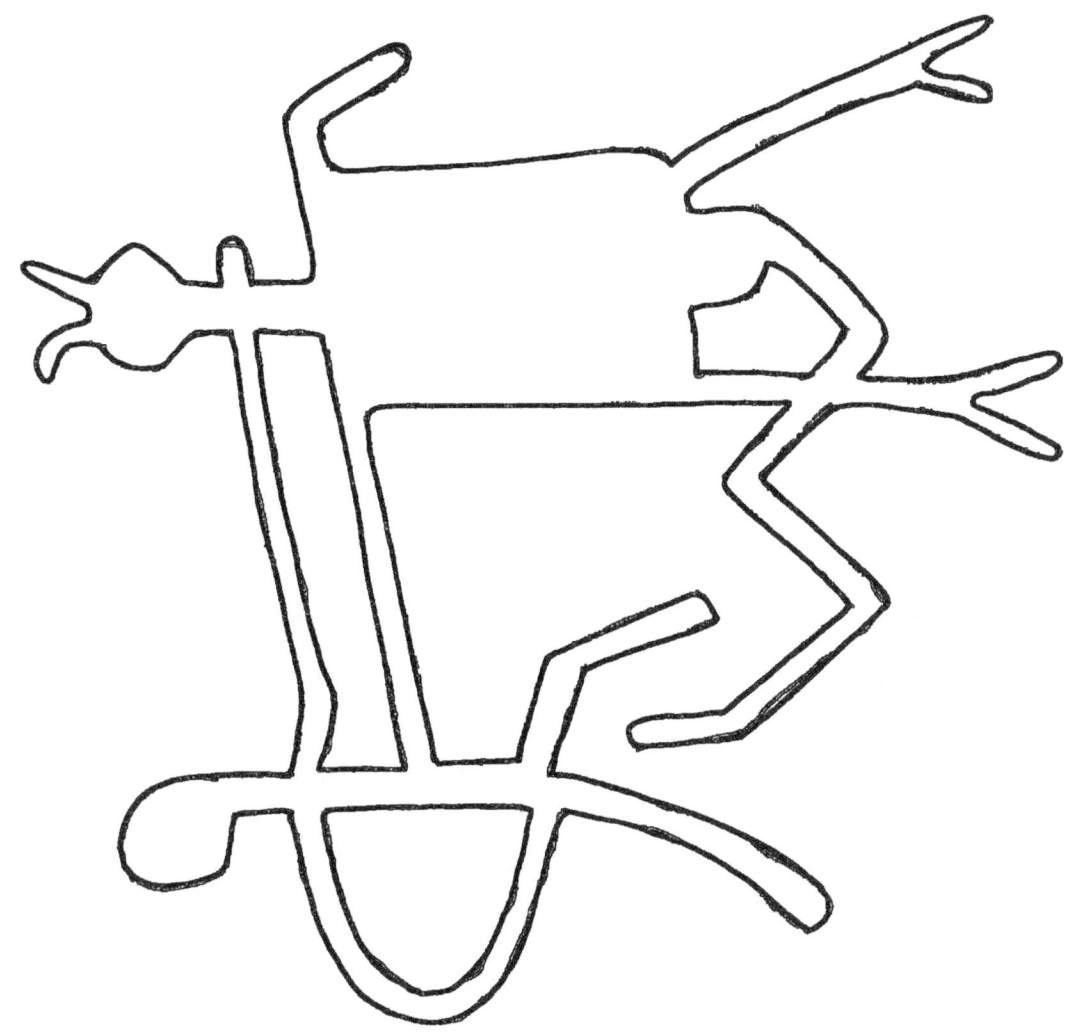

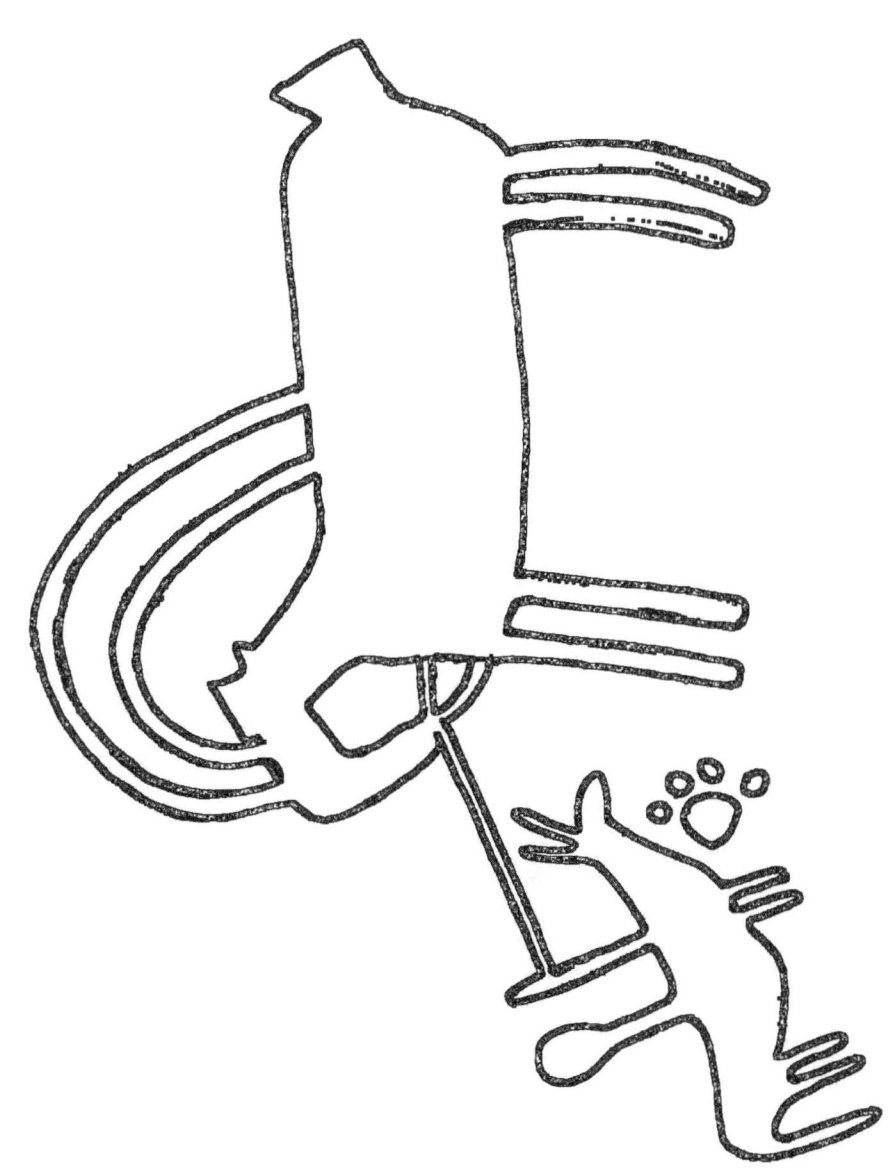

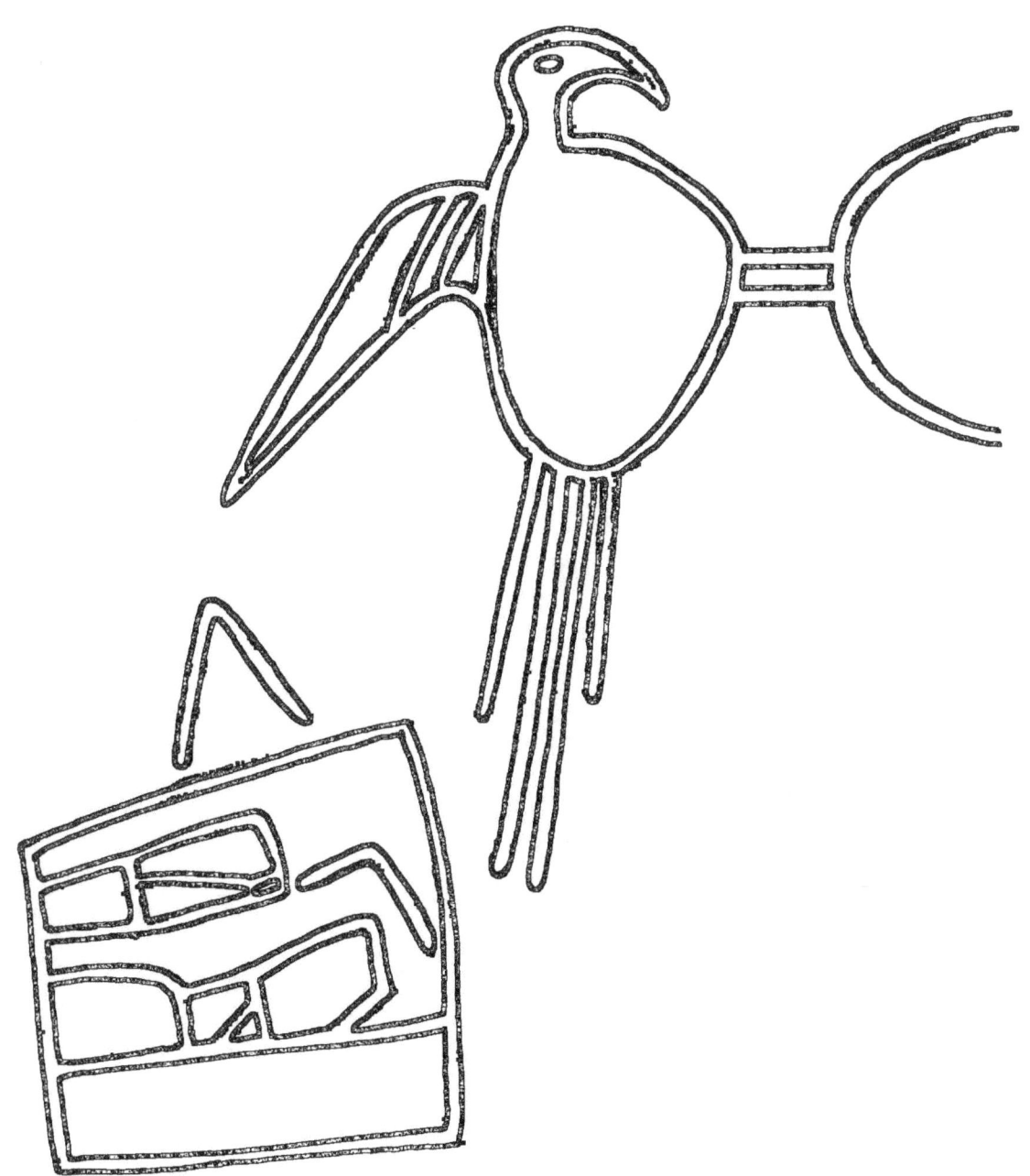

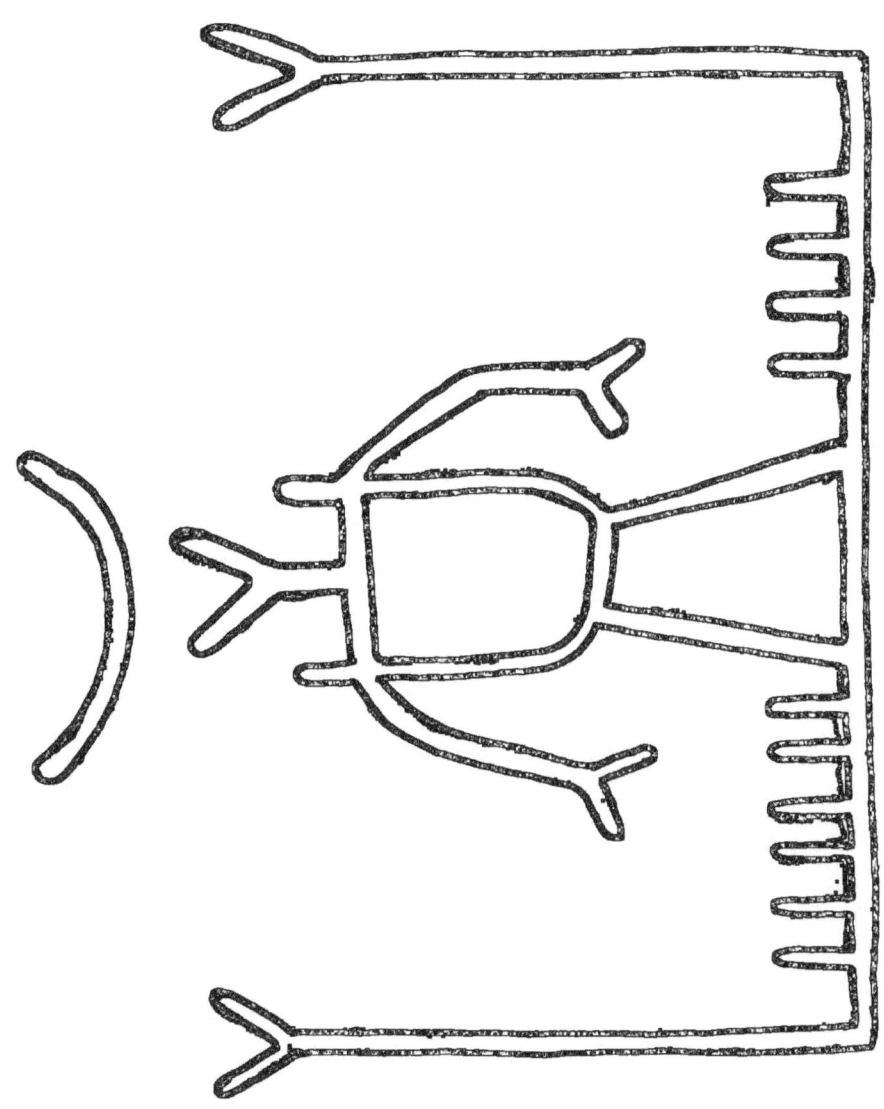

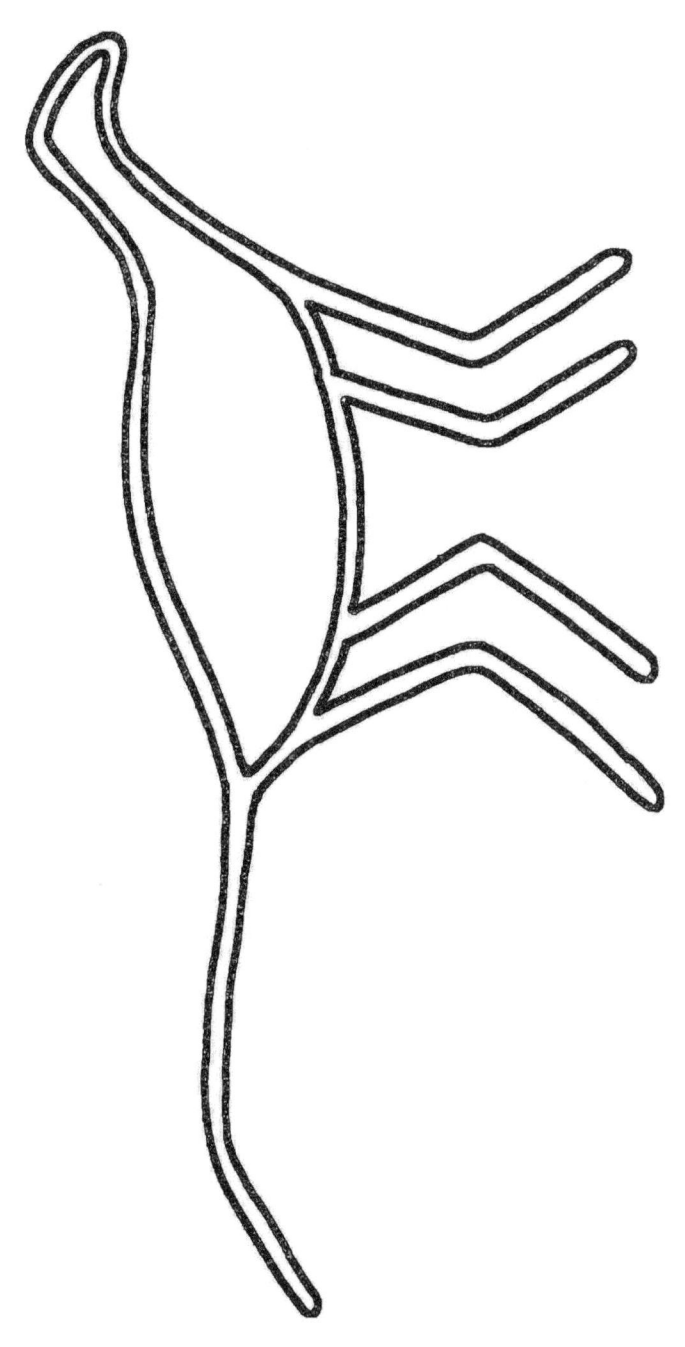

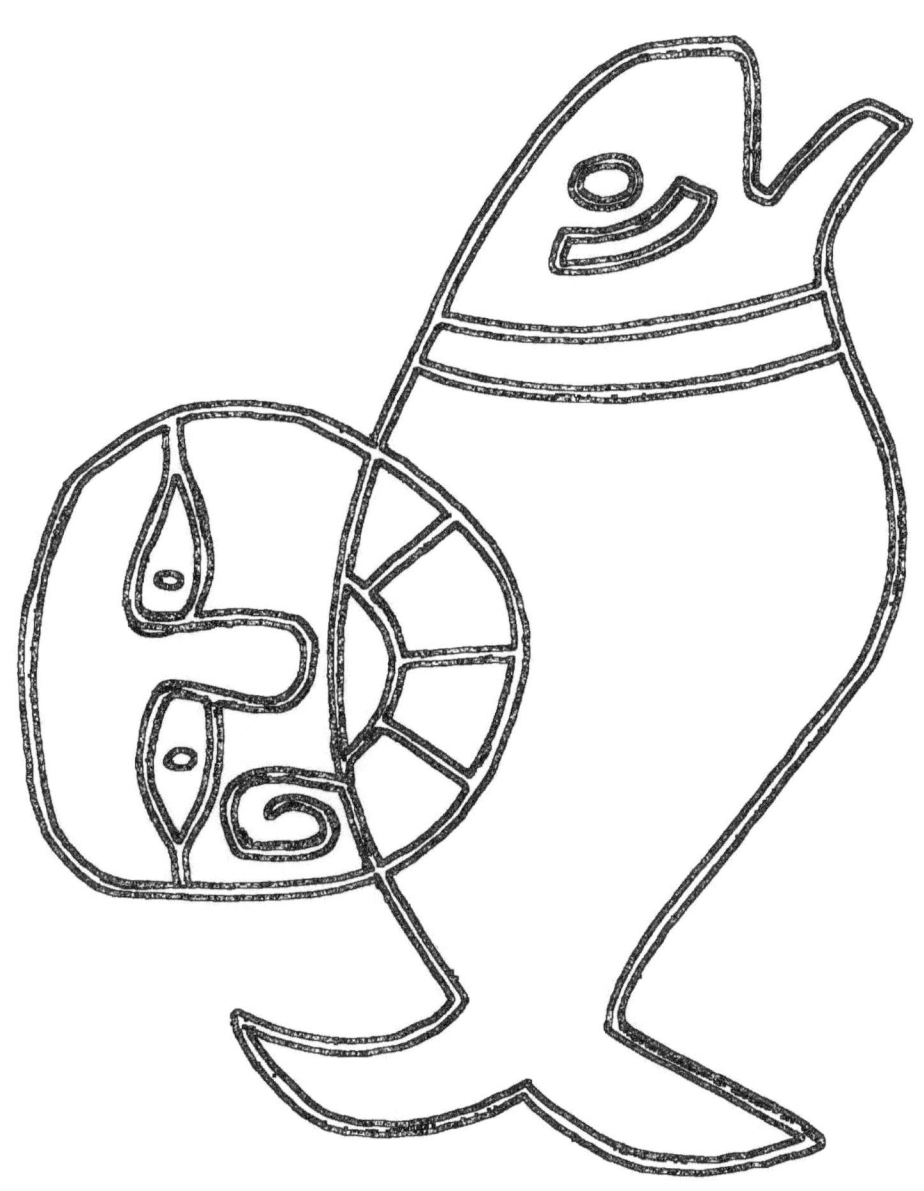

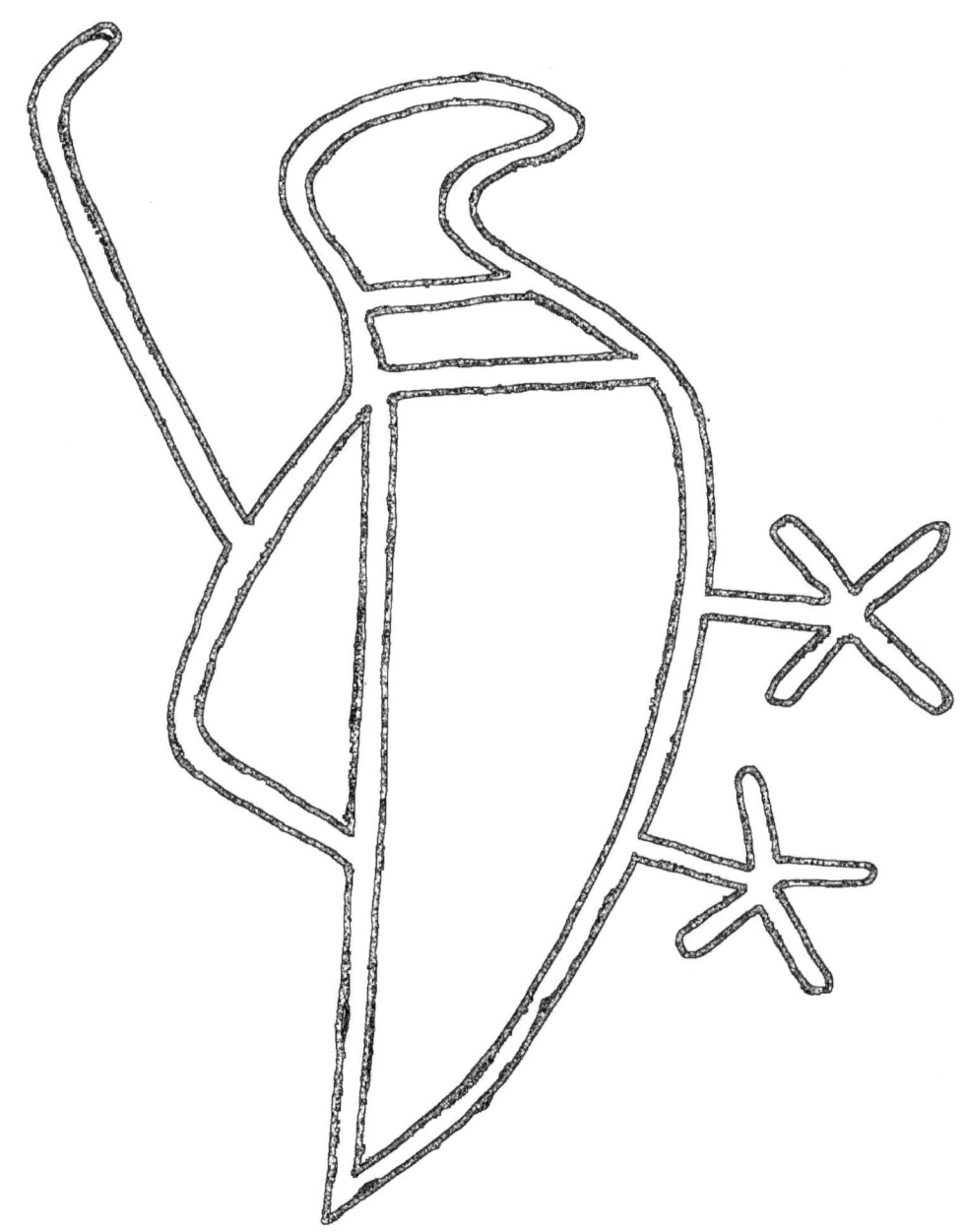

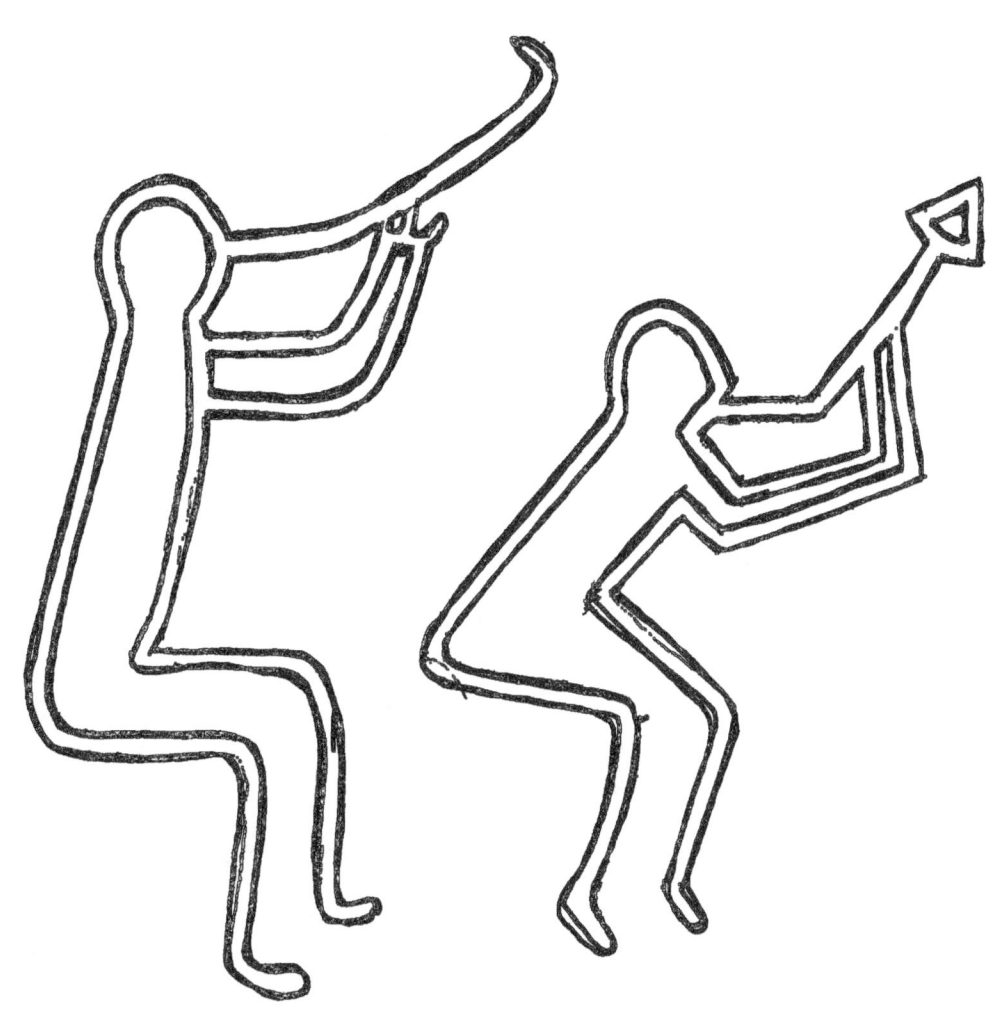

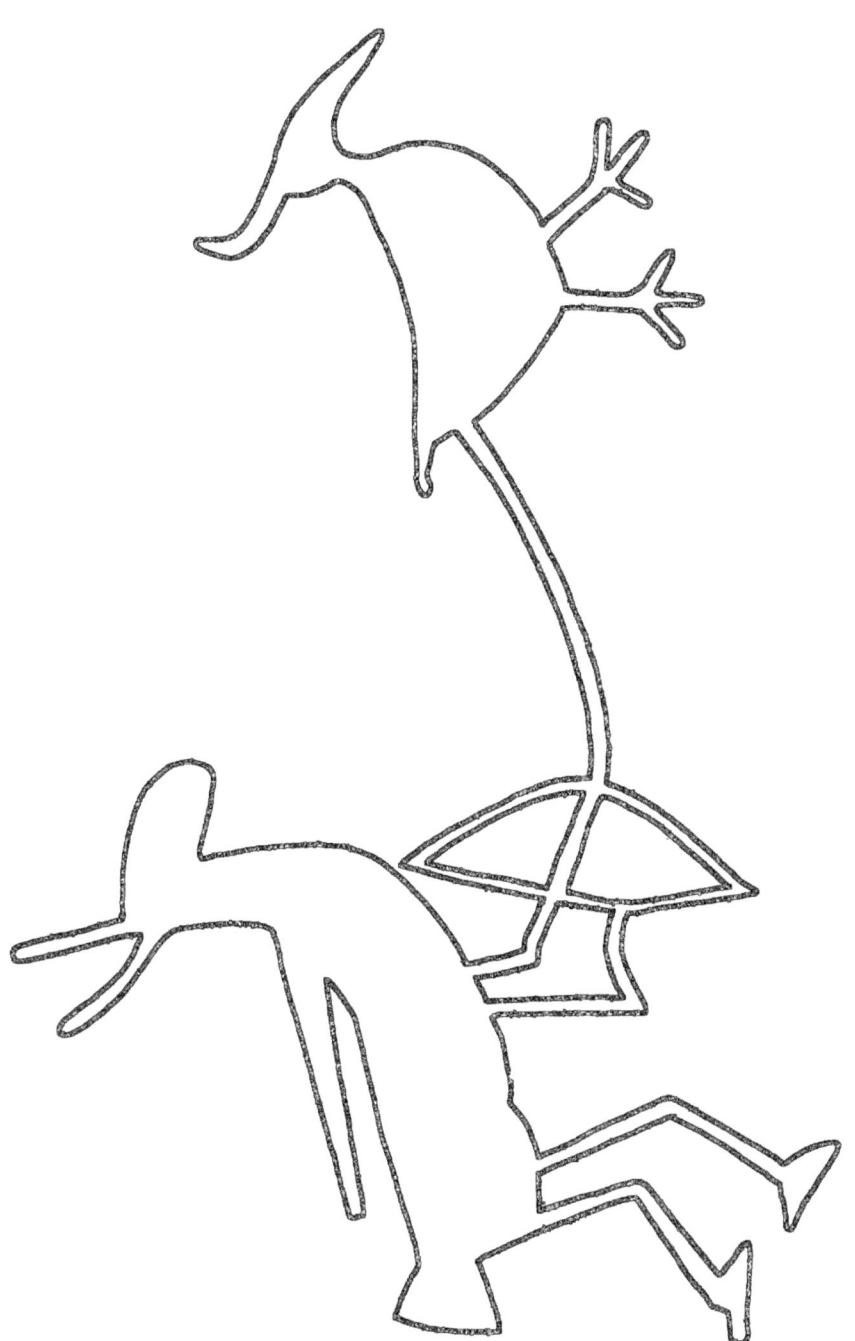

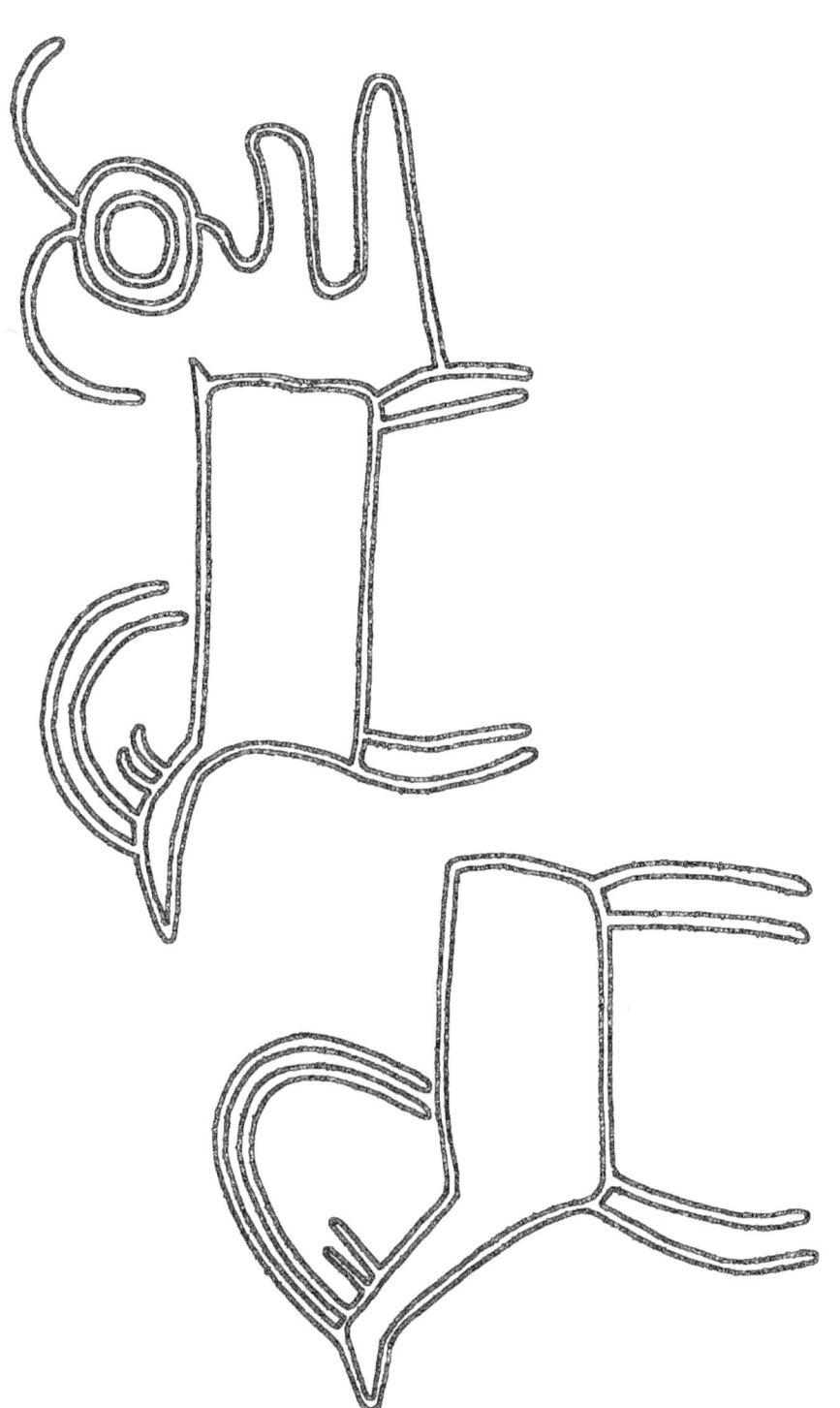

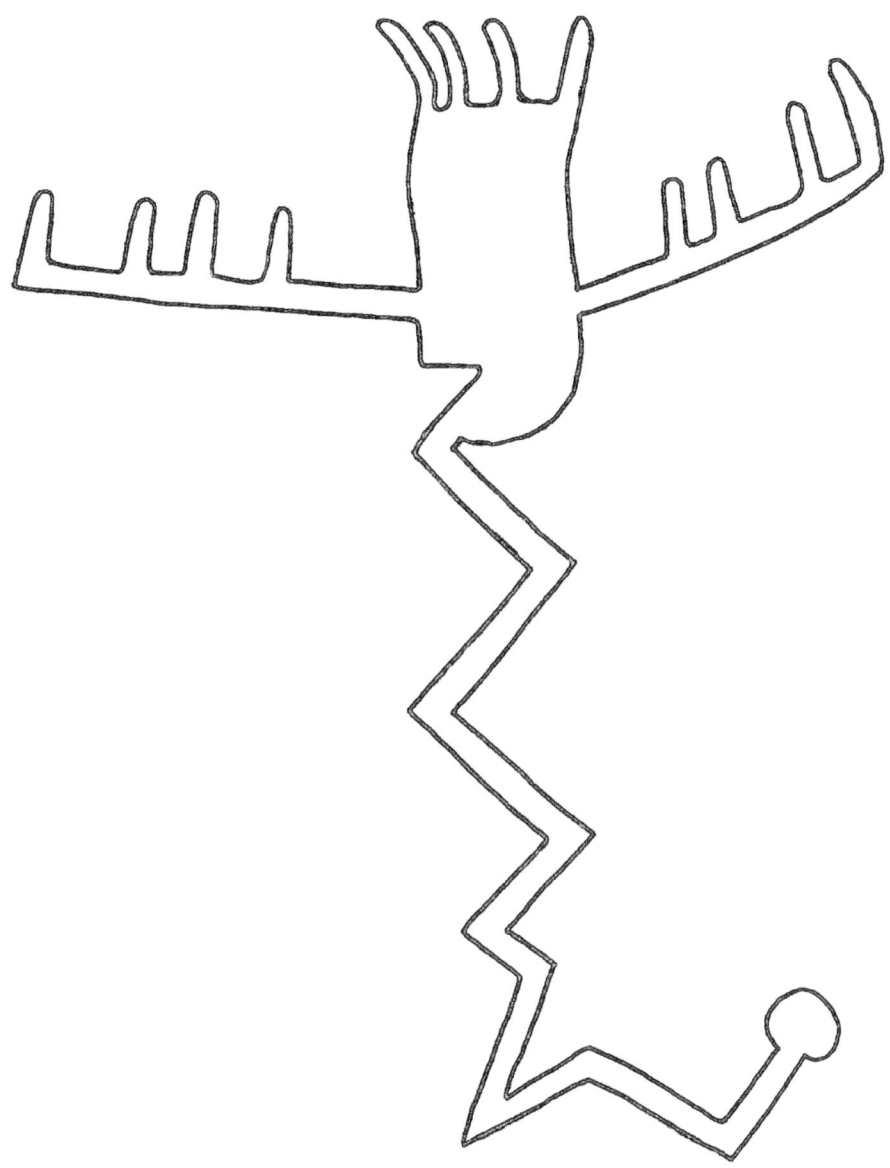

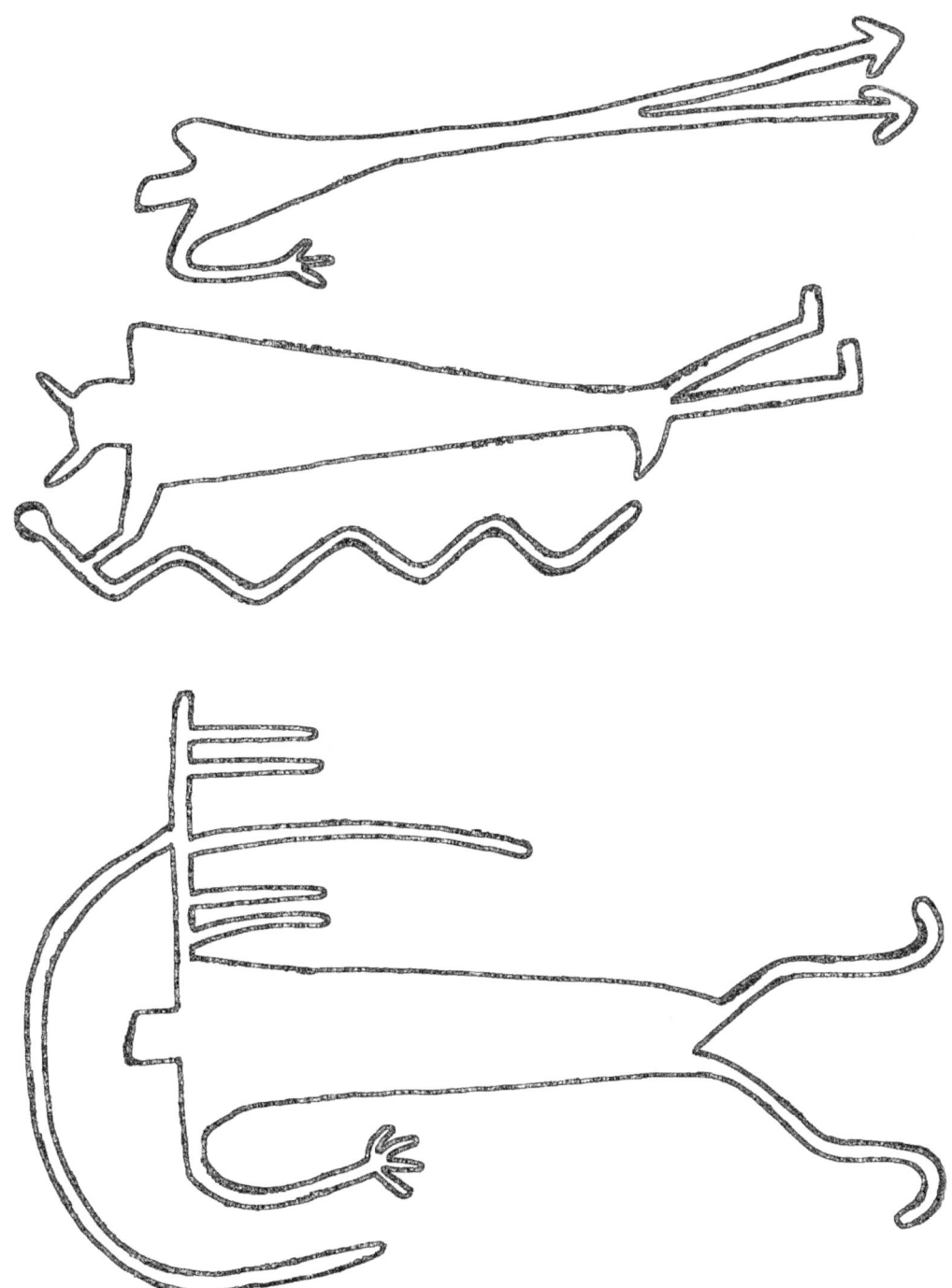

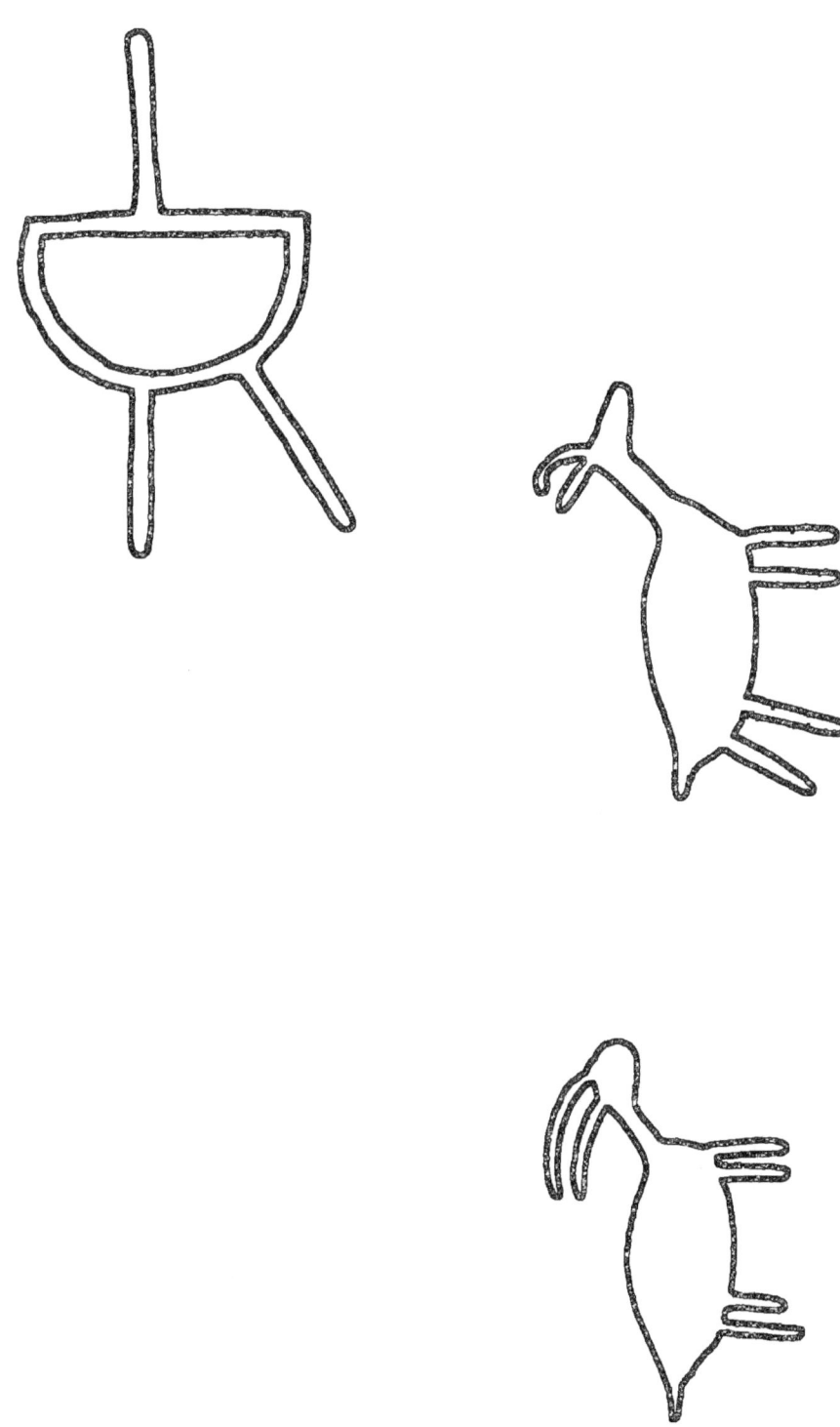

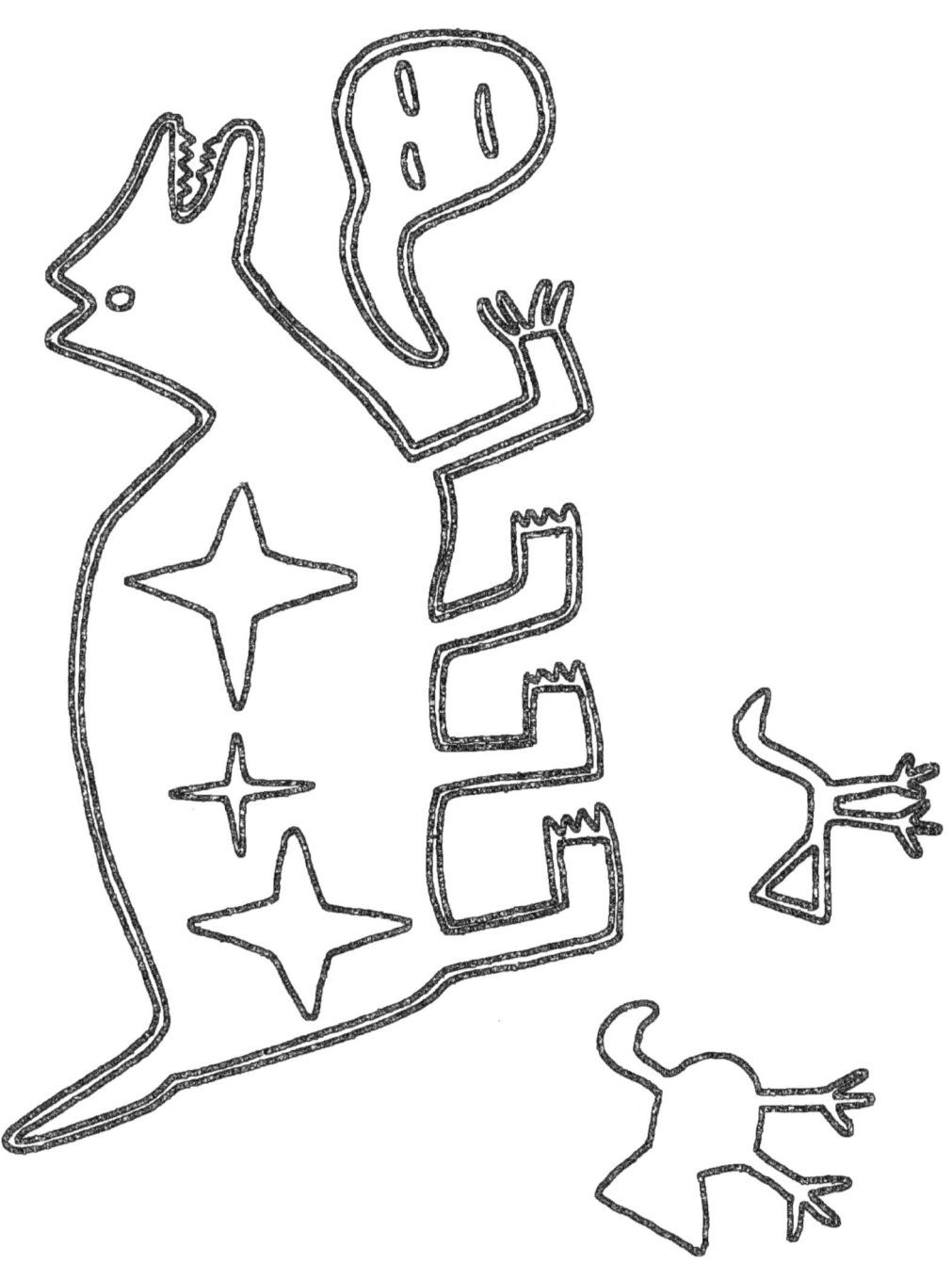

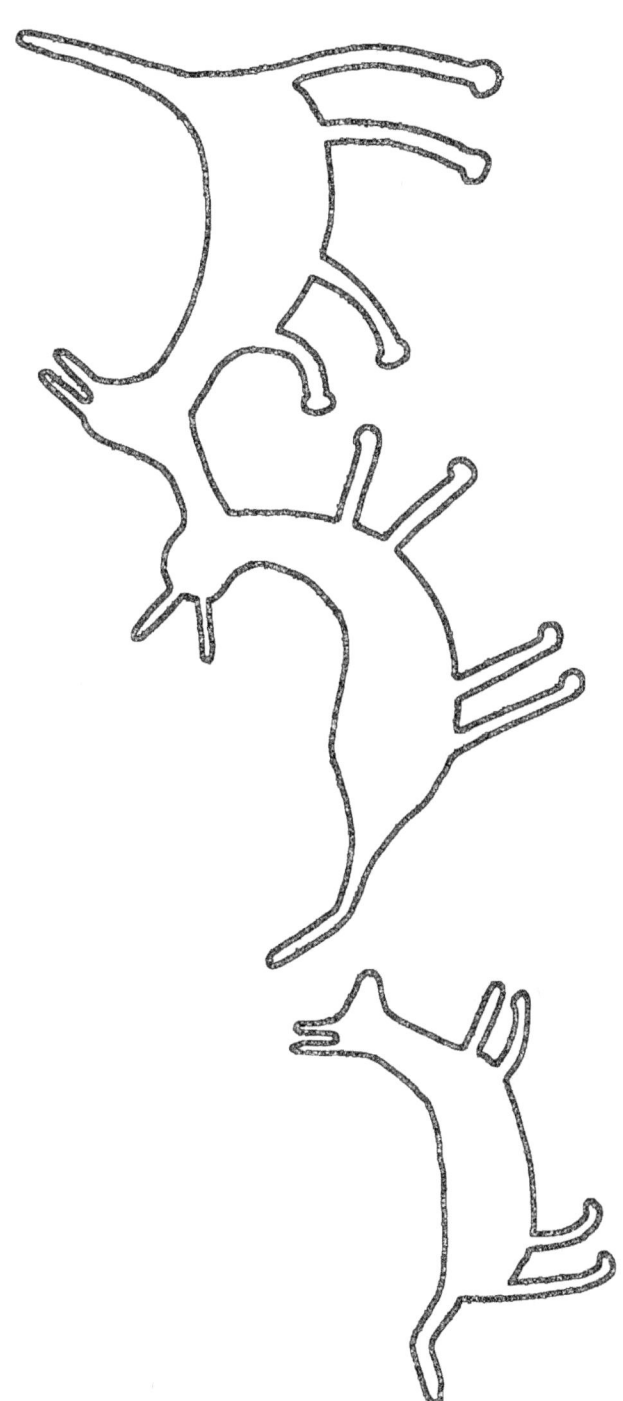

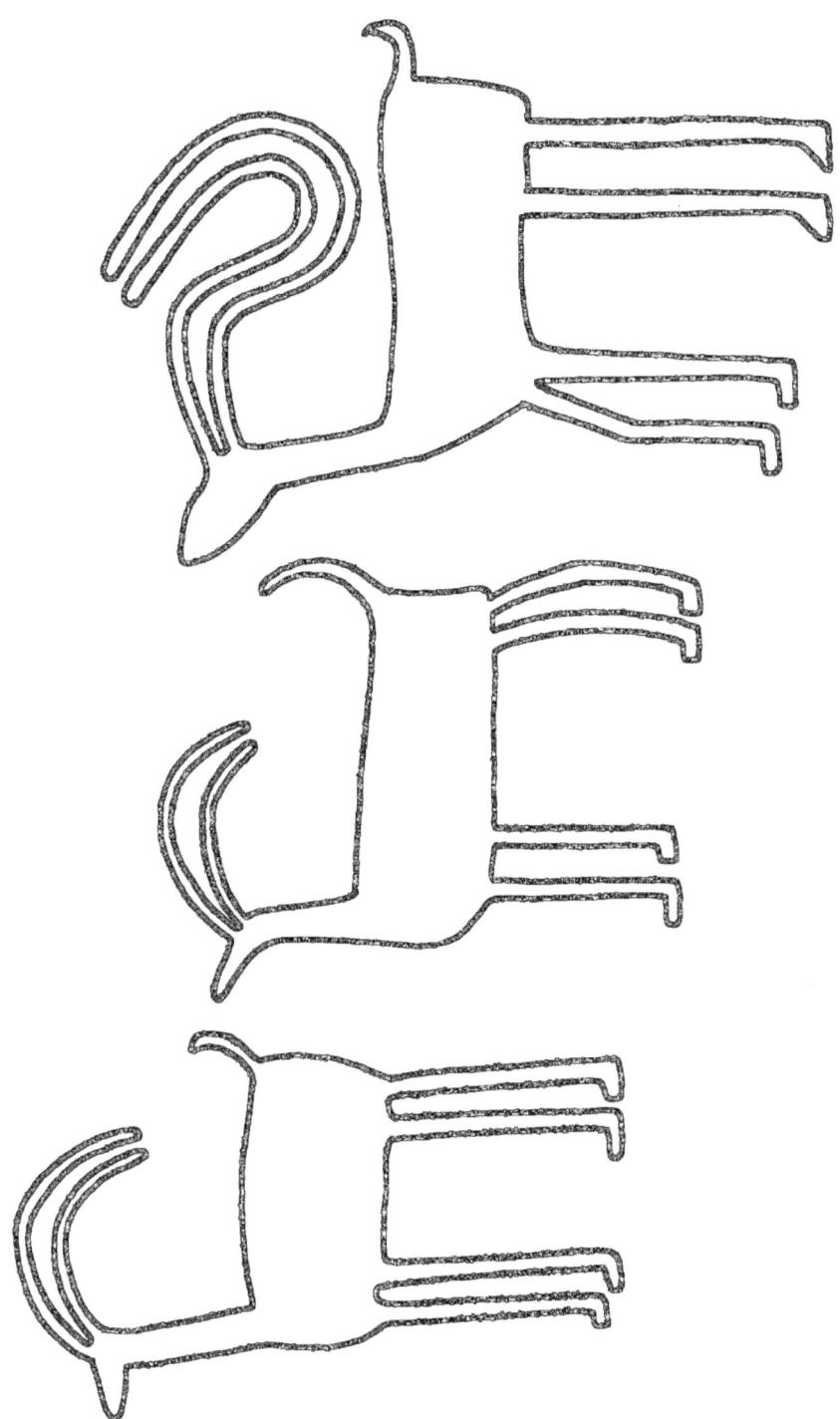

Following are four renderings I did with variegated backgrounds. Add color to these pages however you wish.

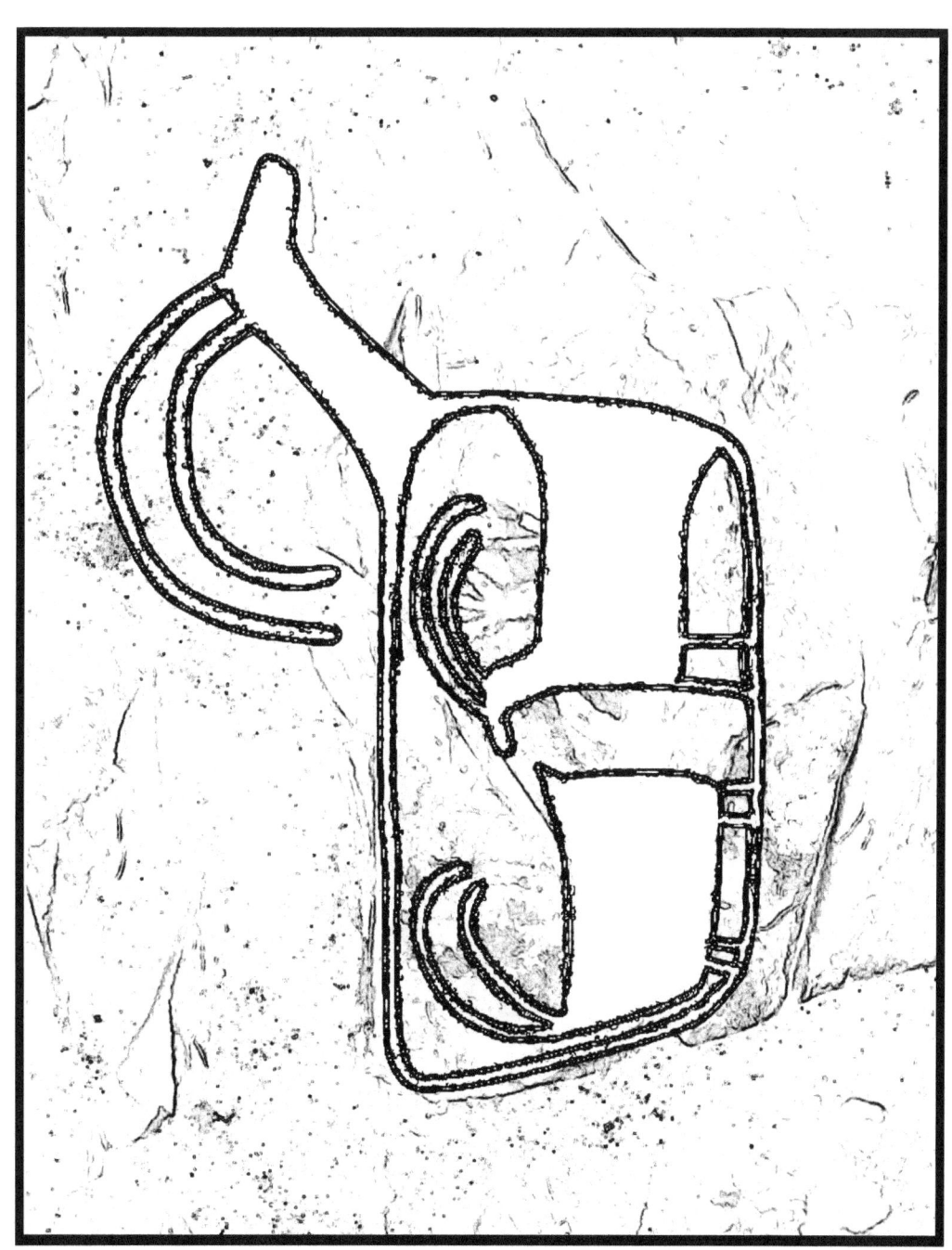

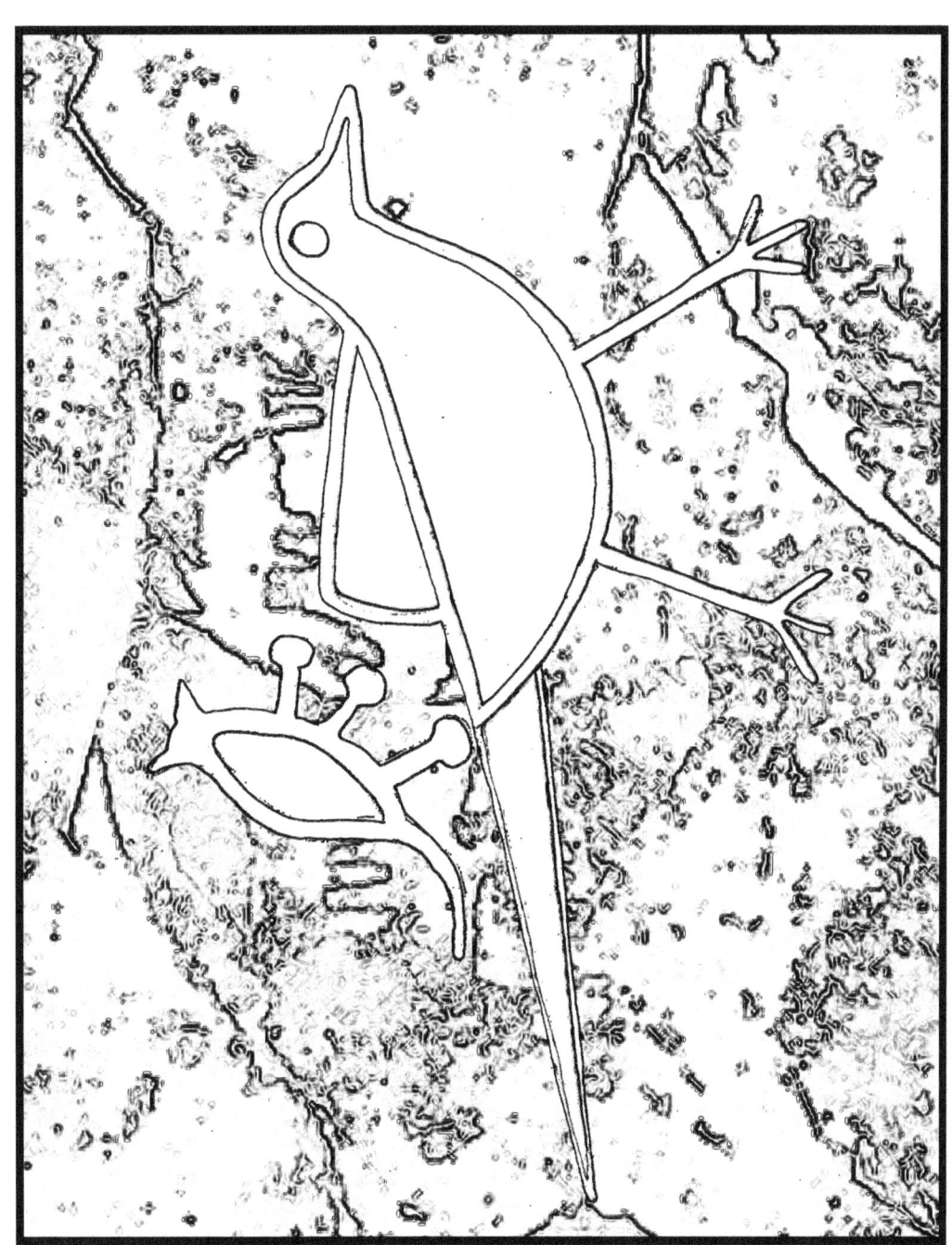

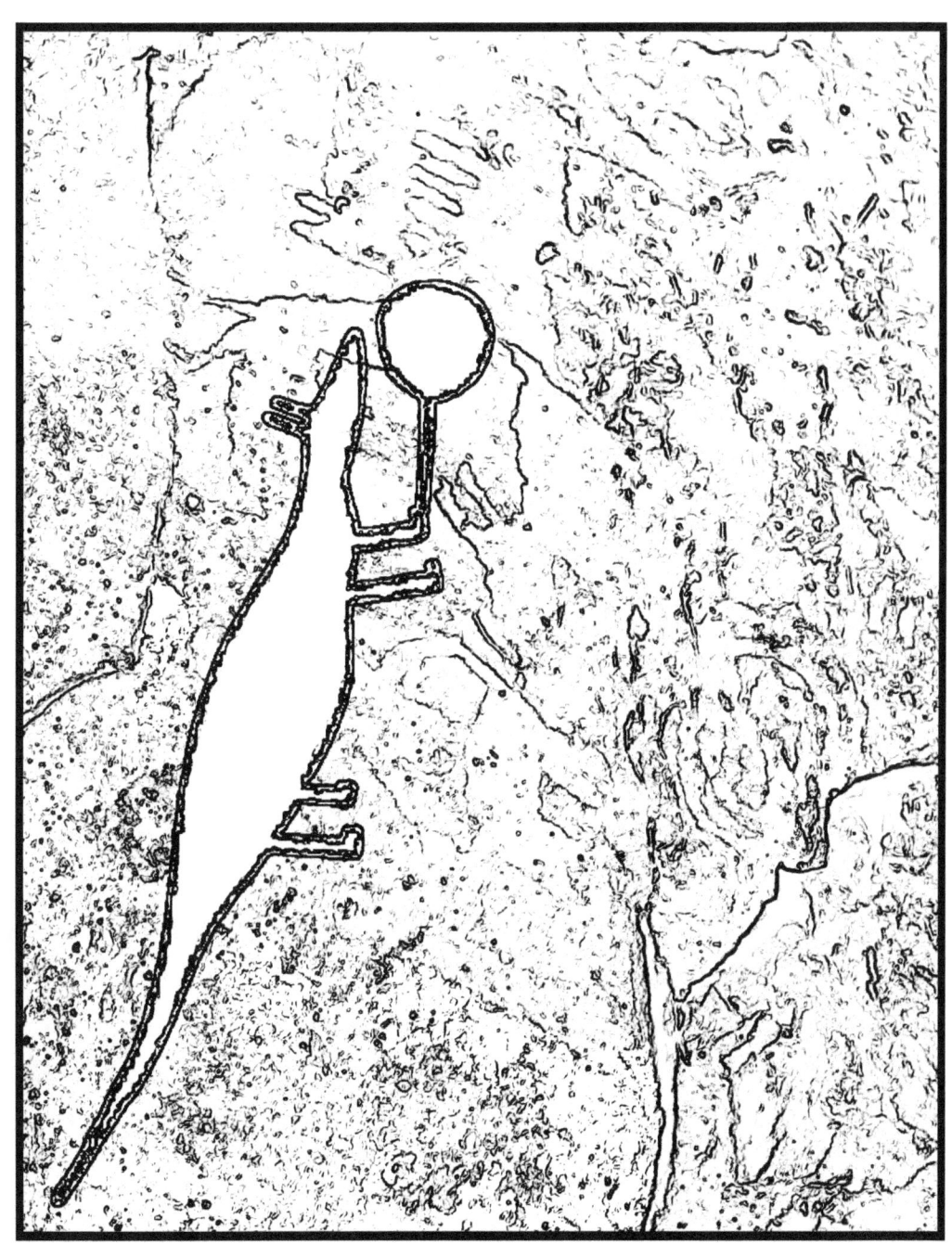

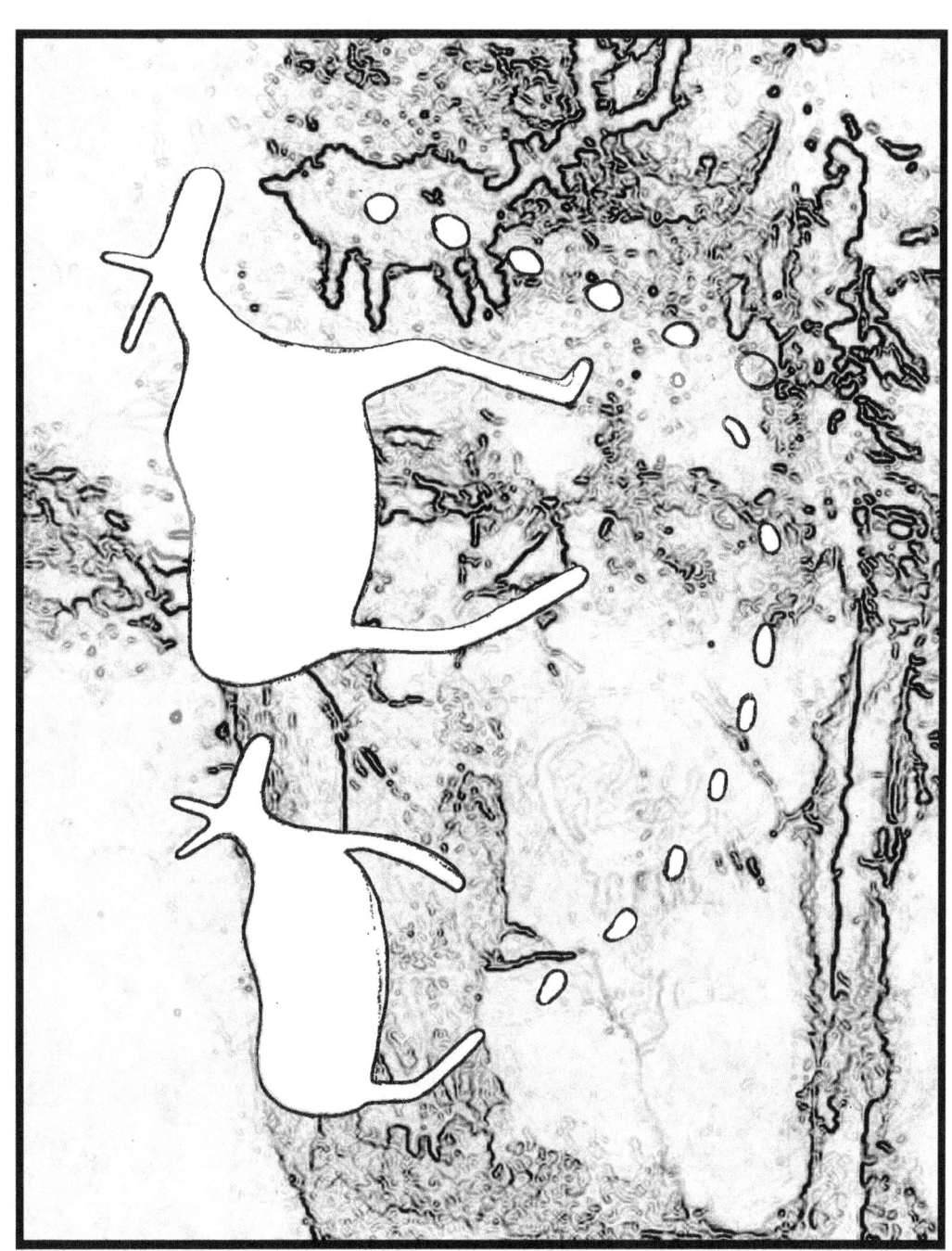

About the drawings in this book

Debbie created the drawings in this coloring book while working on her master's thesis in Archeology. Debbie loved to laugh and her good humor is imbued in the line drawings she made of the petroglyphs. She drew them to take her mind off things and to relieve stress. She was playing, not working. She just looked in books and at pictures and made these wonderful line drawings. She sent them to me and I used the images to make a set of encaustic paintings.

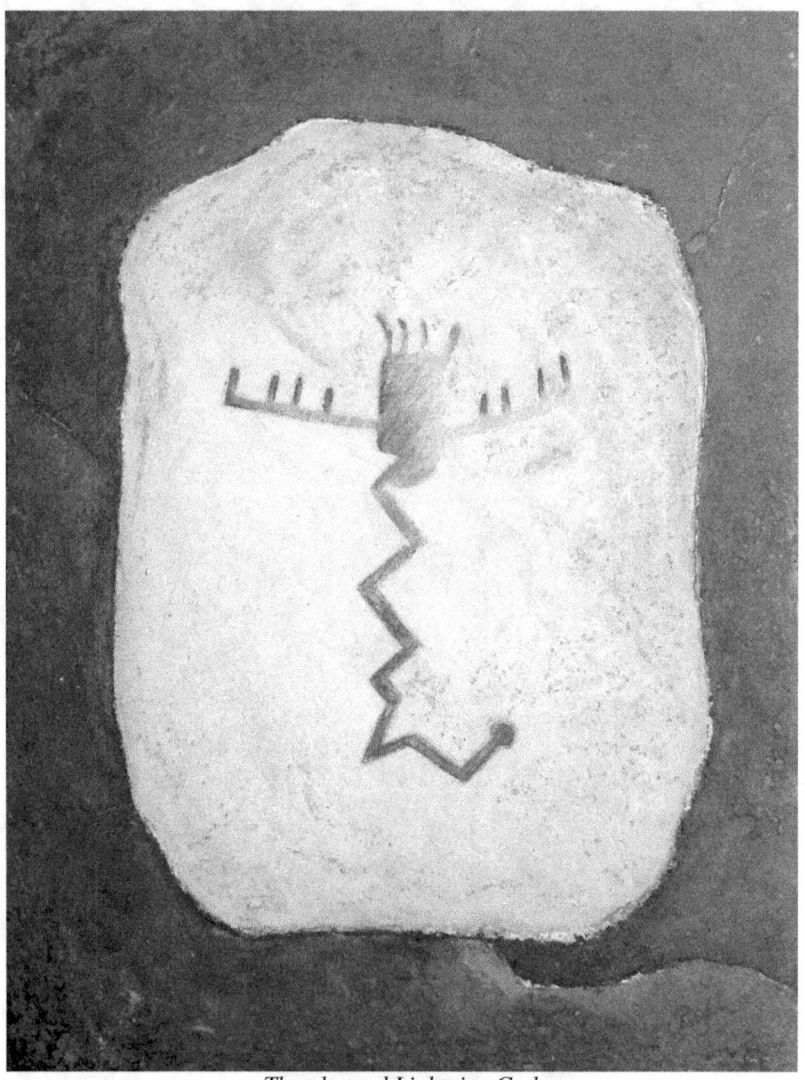

Thunder and Lightning God
15" x 11"
Encaustic on paper

After working with the Thunder and Lightning God image I broke free of the flat, rectangular picture plane and started to tear the paper to look like broken pieces of rock. That's when I started to wonder about the impact the petroglyphs were having on my work.

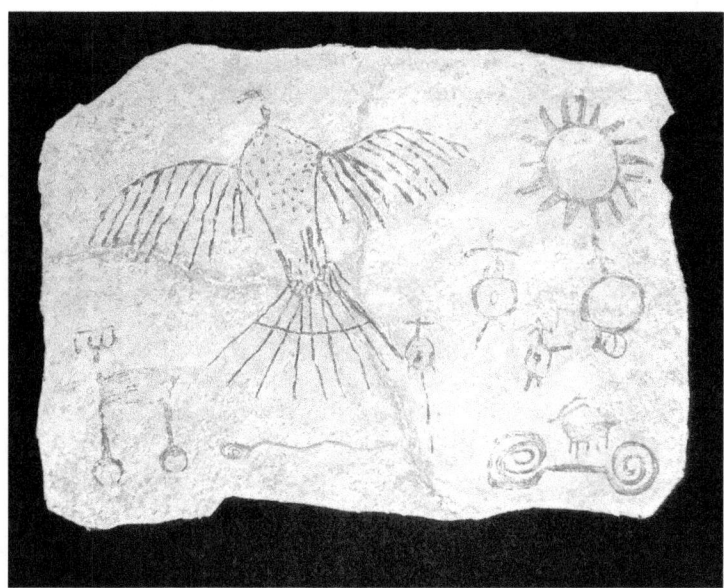

Phoenix with Pumice Marks
11" x 15"
Encaustic on torn paper

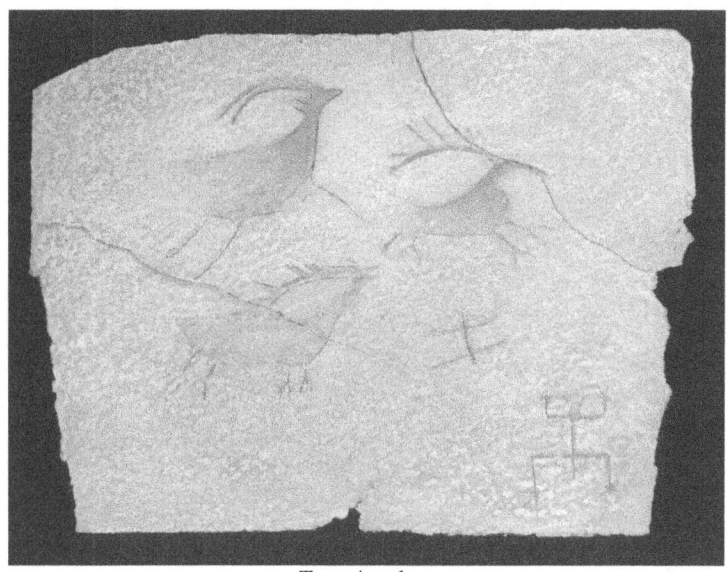

Torn Antelope
11" x 15"
Encaustic on torn paper

Over the twenty years that have passed since Debbie first sent her drawings to me I have worked many times with the petroglyph images. At the very end of the first stint with the images, I saw the following image in my mind's eye. I call it "Spirit Fire" and it is a snapshot of an initiation where the apprentice is being prepared by the shaman to go through a crack into the interior of the cave to receive what teachings might be transmitted from the spirit world. In this picture you can only see the shadows of the figures reflected on the walls of the cave.

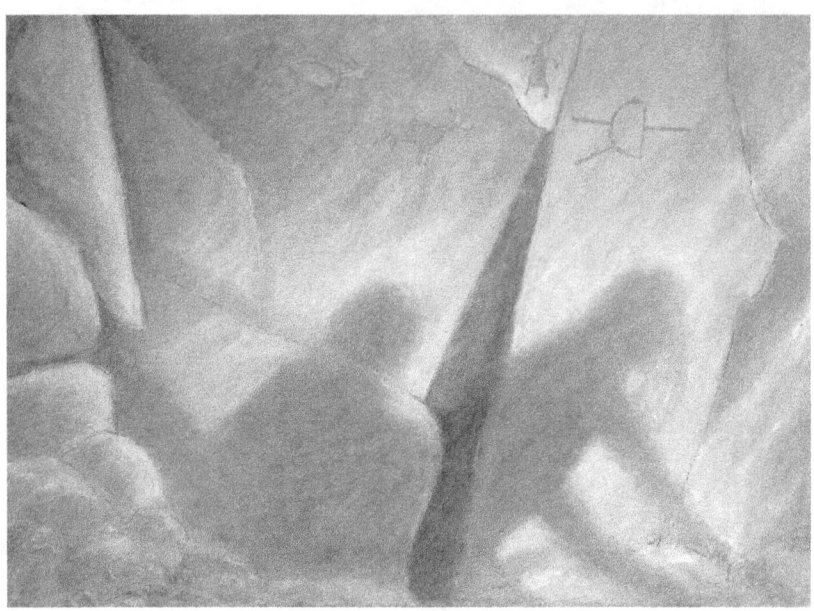

Spirit Fire
11" x 15"
Encaustic on paper

Deborah Lynn Harmon
(1952-2012)

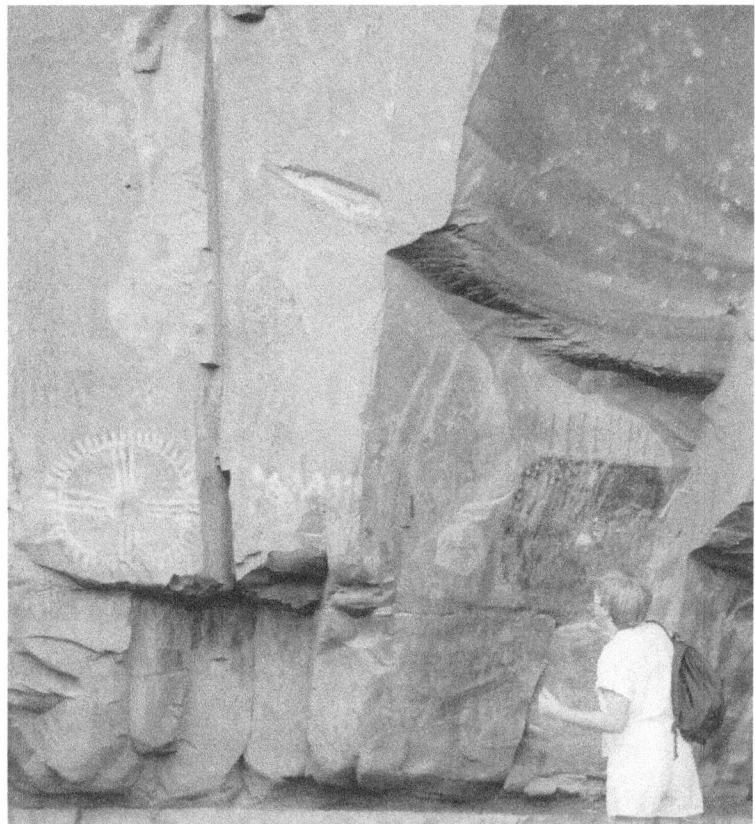

Debbie viewing the cliff carvings at the Palatki Ruins.

Debbie was an archeologist but she didn't much like going on digs. She felt that the living conditions in those places were never very much fun. She was, however, very good at writing grants. Before her untimely death in 2012 she had raised over $8 million for other archeologists to go on digs.

Just before she died she was working up the idea of making a petroglyph coloring book. I was helping her with it. This publication is a tribute to her artistic talent.

A beloved friend for many years, she is missed by all who knew her.